Virginia's Diary

Virginia's Diary

Robin and Virginia Frith

A young family's voyage of discovery – from Boston to Sydney (via Europe) – in a single-engine Cessna

ISBN 978-1-4476-4711-9

Dedication

To Virginia, an extraordinary wife and mother, without whose support and talent in helping me envision and plan this trip, the adventures in this book would not have been possible. She was struck down in her prime by cancer at forty-six, just as she felt she had finished providing the strong guidance, nurturing, and encouragement that set the foundation for our children's lives. She would have been proud of their achievements to date and of the development of her grandchildren.

Contents

Preface

Since 1928, there have been 277 round-the-world trips completed with a light aircraft; 28 of them were before we flew in 1975. More than 70 pilots flew solo; 143 flew in single-engine *planes*[1].

Most of the pre-1975 adventurers who travelled around the world (or even part-way around) before 1975 flew in 2–4 seat planes – primarily because they use less fuel and go farther, even though they are slightly less safe than a twin-engine aircraft.

Although GPS was available for military aircraft from the late 1960s, it wasn't until a large commercial passenger plane – Korean Air Lines Flight 007 – was shot down by the Soviet Air Force on September 1, 1983, after it had strayed from its flight path over the Sea of Japan, that the US Government made GPS available to all private and commercial aircraft.

Before GPS, aircraft in the developed world (especially in the United States, Europe, Canada, and Australia) used VHF radio navigation aids near population centres, but over remote areas and in less-developed nations, pilots had to rely on radio and magnetic compasses or dead reckoning, using compass and stopwatch. In planning such a trip, particularly in a single-engine aircraft, the risks that run through people's minds include power loss in mid-air, the danger of being shot down over almost any foreign air space, and, simply, the challenges of travelling to and from small airports safely with a family. When Virginia and Robin first came up with the idea in 1974 to attempt such a trip, they recognized some of the risks, but the lure of the challenge was too great to resist.

Today, about six adventurers every year take on the same challenge, and many others attempt shorter flights, but it's a far more cautious business. Even though GPS has made flying much safer, pilots are less

---

[1] See FAI – *Federation Aeronautique Internationale* www.fai.org – the governing body for air sports and aeronautical world records.

naïve about what might go wrong. Overall, this makes the cost prohibitive for most, mainly because of insurance, not to mention fuel. Unless trips are undertaken by wealthy individuals, they need sponsorship. Many adventurers also feel safer travelling in convoy with an experienced team – such as with a group called AirJourney that organizes an Around-the-world Air *Rally*[2].

But perhaps as a result of today's heightened understanding of the risks, in particular after 9/11, we have been unable to find records of any other family having attempted this trip since Virginia, Robin, and family completed it in 1975. The only available record of a family flying even the equivalent of halfway around the world in recent years is of the Wagners from Denmark who, in 2005, with five family members on board (including pre-teen children), travelled from the top of Norway south across the Mediterranean and North Africa to the southern tip of South Africa and back again up the west *coast*[3].

The early '70s was a unique time in history because it was both likely and possible for a family to attempt such a trip. Light aircraft with the capacity to carry a family had become affordable and proven to be reasonably safe. Cessna built its reputation for safe and reliable travel with its fleet of simple, low-cost, and easy-to-fly craft, starting with the 172 and 182 in the 1960s. By the 1970s, more than one hundred thousand Cessna planes were flying and had covered millions of miles. In 1962, the Cessna 206 was introduced. Its rugged construction and large cabin made it popular as the 'station wagon of the air'. Because of this, the Frith family chose the C206 for their trip, stock-standard straight off the assembly line at the Cessna *factory*[4].

---

[2] See http://www.airjourney.com/blog/?page_id=2 for details of this organization. See also www.soloflights.org and www.earthrounders.com.

[3] See http://www.flyingfamilytour.dk for details

[4] The only concession was extra fuel tanks to provide a very conservative margin of safety for the longest legs of the trip – an additional 100 gallons (380 litres) for thirteen hours' endurance over the North Atlantic and 30 gallons (114 litres) for eight hours' endurance for the rest of the trip. In the event of a ditching in water, we carried an inflatable life-raft, life vests, wetsuits, and a floatable EPIRB (electronic distress beacon).

Although the C206 cabin is quite spacious (about the same size as a medium-sized station wagon) with, normally, six seats (three rows of two) and a large cargo bay behind the rear seats, the touring needs of a family of five ensured that the cabin was filled to capacity. The touring load included: a thirty-gallon fuel tank, occupying the space of a seat; one backpack for each member of the family; four fold-up bicycles, one with a

The mid-1970s was a time of optimism: the economic outlook was bright, and the global conflicts associated with this new and modern world had abated with the conclusion of the Vietnam War and the lessening of Middle East tensions. The price of oil came back to 'normal', and the impact of the recession of 1971–1972 had diminished so that this trip did not feel like an extravagance or folly but a celebration of what was possible.

My father and mother, as you will see from this journal, simply saw this as an opportunity to pack their bags and bikes in an aircraft and take the ultimate family trip around the world.

Angela Frith – February 2011

---

children's seat over the rear wheel; flight safety and navigation gear such as books and maps; extra clothes; and children's books.

Our routine while touring Europe was to land at our day's destination, pack our backpacks with the requirements for the number of days to be spent in that town, and unpack the bikes and peddle into town to look for suitable accommodation. Airports tend to be quite a distance out of town, so some of our rides were very long. We tended not to pre-book accommodation as that would have forced a fixed itinerary, which was not a good idea while having to cope with variable flying conditions.

Introduction

It's 11.30 a.m., on October 7, 1975, and I have my single-engine Cessna 206 lined up for departure on runway 11 at Tehran International Airport for the next stop on our extensive journey through eighteen countries and thirty-eight cities/towns, from Boston in the United States to Sydney, Australia.

With me in the cabin are my wife, Virginia, and our three children, Angela, ten; Stuart, eight; and Rowena, five.

As well as the family, the cabin is fully packed with the touring luggage for five, a 30-gallon (114-litre) auxiliary fuel tank, an inflatable life raft, life preservers for five, an electronic distress beacon, and four fold-up bicycles. With full fuel in the tanks, this load brings the aircraft up to its maximum legal take-off weight of 3,600 lbs (1,633 kg).

Directly ahead of us is one of the most daunting legs of our trip with a one-stop flight from Tehran to Karachi over some of the most inhospitable areas of the earth – the Dasht-e Kavir (Great Salt Desert) and the Dasht-e Lut (Emptiness Desert). This is a 1,000-mile (1,620-km) stretch of desert from Tehran to Zahedan, which is located on the south-east border of Iran, adjacent to the junction of the Afghanistan and Pakistan borders.

With take-off clearance from the Tehran tower, we are soon airborne on a south-easterly heading and a dead reckoning course to Zahedan. We will rely on our magnetic compass and estimated ground speed to find the small re-fuelling stop on the edge of the desert.

As we turn on course and reach our cruising altitude of 10,000 ft., below us, we have already entered the desert, with sand waves and hills all the way to the horizon.

After six hours of this desolate landscape and, fortunately, fine clear weather, a few buildings appear on the horizon then the flashing of the rotating light beacon on top of the tower as the airport at Zahedan comes into sight.

A smooth touchdown and taxi up to the terminal building and another leg of our journey comes to a successful conclusion.

How did my family and I come to be on the edge of the great Iranian Desert in a heavily loaded single-engine light aircraft en route to Sydney?

What events led up to the decision to attempt to fly my family on a journey most of the way around the world, and what experiences did we have along the way?

What effect did this adventure have on the lives of the three young children who actively participated in the journey?

This book is not just another around-the-world flying adventure story by an experienced solo pilot. It is the story of a family's flying journey around the world seen through the eyes of not just the pilot but through the eyes of all members of the family, especially, posthumously, the astute observations of Virginia.

Virginia's diary entries, written while in the co-pilot's seat on the long flight legs and while waiting in the numerous third-world airport facilities for her husband to complete customs and immigration procedures and to file the flight plans, accurately detail the family's activities on the journey and provide a unique perspective on her husband's flying and the various tourist activities undertaken by the family on the journey.

Take-off

At 10.30 a.m. on Friday August 1, 1975, with Tom Stockebrand in the co-pilot's seat, I start the engine of the Cessna 206 and taxi out on runway 3 at MinuteMan Air Field, near Boston in the north-eastern United States.

For the trip across the North Atlantic, because of fuel, safety, and loading requirements, we have decided that Virginia and the kids will fly commercial direct to Shannon in Ireland while I am joined by Tom as we navigate our way up the east coast of the United States and Canada, around the Arctic Circle, and over the northern tip of the Atlantic Ocean to Shannon, where Tom will leave the adventure and the family will join me on the ride of our lives.

Figure 1 Preparing for departure from MinuteMan.

I wave goodbye to Virginia, Angela, Stuart, and Rowena, and various other friends, and, with only half of the fuel capacity loaded and ten degrees of flaps, we make a short take-off and climb on course for Manchester, New Hampshire, under a *VFR*[i] flight plan. That was to be our first stop on the first leg of our first family flight across the world.

Tom Stockebrand was a fellow engineer at Digital Equipment Corporation and a licensed pilot with considerably more flying experience than I had. It was good to have him in the co-pilot's seat on this challenging leg of the journey, not just as a back-up pilot should I become indisposed but also for us to cross check each other on the dead reckoning navigation and other flying decisions that needed to be made.

Tom remembers:

"When Robin phoned me to ask whether I wanted to go on this trip, I gave his question a long pause as my mind whirled around, and then said, "Yes!" I realised that such an opportunity for adventure would never be dropped in my lap again."

At Manchester, we pick up the final *ADF*[ii] radio and adjust the accuracy of our magnetic compass with the aircraft configured for extended range flying. It's barely a fifteen-minute flight at 2,000 ft., and we land and taxi to Stead Avionics to pick up the ADF. With a little help, we swing the compass and are taxiing out for departure within thirty minutes of touching down, cleared on *IFR*[iii] (instrument flight rules) for Moncton, in the province of New Brunswick, Canada.

We climb to 7000 ft, expecting clear but hazy conditions for most of the trip. I don't like the rushed departure, but if we aren't away quickly, we'll be cutting it fine getting into Moncton by the time they close at 4 p.m. local time, one hour ahead of Boston.

As we climb, Tom calculates our ETA (estimated time of arrival) at Moncton right at 4 p.m. It will be tight, but we should make it on time. Tom is clearly nervous about the forthcoming flight over the North Atlantic, telling me as we fly up the coast of Maine that he has packed a wetsuit in case of engine failure over the Arctic waters. 'How are you going to put on a wetsuit in the cabin,' I ask him. 'I'll find a way,' he replies. I let it drop as I did not want to think about the possibility that it could happen.

Moncton is where we will request clearance from the Canadian Department of Civil Aviation for the trans-Atlantic crossing. Canada has responsibility for search and rescue operations over the western portion of the North Atlantic – remember the Titanic? – so they are very keen to ensure we have an airworthy aircraft, are equipped with the necessary navigation and communications equipment, and have on board life-saving gear and an emergency radio transmitter which will float in the sea and power up of its own accord.

We level off at 7000 ft., tune in the Augusta *VOR*[iv] (VHF omnidirectional range), lock in our autopilot, and settle back to observe the beautiful but rugged Maine coast as we cruise along in calm conditions.

During our five-year family sojourn in the United States, Maine was one of our favourite holiday destinations, both in summer with its lush green deciduous and evergreen vegetation and, particularly, in the fall (autumn) with the magnificent bright orange, red, and yellow leaves on the trees as they prepared for their winter.

Off the coast we see Monhegan Island, and I relate to Tom a piece of family folklore. Virginia and I visited Monhegan Island in 1964 for a lobster bake about nine months before my eldest daughter, Angela, was born. Angela's second name is Monhegan, and, as a result, it has been the source of some amusement to the other two siblings as they grow up.

Bangor VOR comes up right on schedule, and the ground speed readout indicates that we should arrive in Moncton at 3.55 p.m. – and so it turns out. Precisely at 3.55 p.m., we taxi from Moncton strip to the airport area, directed by ground control, for the checkout of trans-Atlantic flights. We run to the customs hall and clear customs in a panic because we're checking into Canada at the same time as we want to check out. But, whew, the Civil Aviation clerk assures us there's no need for concern about timing. He even calls the officials from downtown Moncton, and they agree to come out in about fifteen minutes to run their eye over us. During that time, we climb the tower to the flight briefing office and file a flight plan to Goose Bay for that night and check the en route weather.

In due course, the Civil Aviation official arrives. Over a cup of coffee in the airport restaurant, we complete a short written questionnaire and oral test on the North Atlantic information and our preparation and knowledge of the route to be flown and the navigation aids and services for that route. He inspects the Cessna and checks the emergency dinghy, lifejackets, and radio beacon. I think the major thing he's checking for is whether we know what we're letting ourselves in for and that we have prepared ourselves thoroughly for the cold Atlantic.

He asks to check the special overweight certification in the Cessna logbook to ensure that the installation had been done and certified in a professional manner.

Eventually, he seems satisfied and signs off our flight plan for the crossing. We taxi down to refuel at the Aero Club, half a mile across the airport, and, for the first time, we fill the aircraft to its 188-gallon maximum capacity (88 in the wing tanks and 100 in the large cabin tank). That's a little over thirteen hours of flight endurance at normal cruising altitude.

As we top up the last inches of the tank, we step back and survey the 206, its tail nearly dragging on the ground as it's now loaded to three hundred pounds over gross weight.

'How's this thing ever going to get off the ground?' I silently wonder. Tom scratches his head too.

With the engine on, we taxi out to runway 29, copy our clearance for Goose Bay, and line up at the end of the 8,000 ft. strip to provide ourselves the maximum distance should the heavy aircraft be reluctant to fly. I can feel the nose in the air, as if it's sniffing the afternoon sky, which is hot and humid.

With full throttle, propeller on fine pitch, and ten degrees of flaps, we commence to roll. It seems to take forever to reach our sixty-five knots rotation speed, but eventually the aircraft struggles into the air and commences a slow climb. A right turn on climb out and we are on course for the Malpeque intercept of air route Red 1 for Goose Bay, leading up over the Gulf of St Lawrence via Gaspe Peninsula and Anticosta Island.

Darkness falls over the Gulf of St Lawrence, and there is a heavy line of thunderstorms ahead on the Newfoundland-Quebec border, with the tops considerably above our cruising altitude of 10,000 ft.

Now, for the first time, we are moving away from the high-density area of radio navigation aids to the more sparsely populated land of radio beacons, the Canadian tundra; we are together and alone in an aircraft out of direct communications range and with no signs of human habitation on the earth below.

How the hell did we get here?

Background

Flying Influences

With a chartered accountant as my father, I could not say that adventure and flying was 'in my blood', but with my two elder brothers involved in the broader aviation industry, I guess they had significant influence. Peter, who was seven years older than me, had a fifty-year career with the Department of Civil Aviation (DCA) in the maintenance of radio communications and navigation aids, and, because of his hobby, he became known as 'Mr Avionics' in Tasmania, as he maintained all the light aircraft and helicopter avionics in this small state.

My earliest recollections of Denis, who is five years older than me, is of him constructing radio-controlled model aircraft when he was ten or eleven – an interest that led him to the study of aeronautical engineering and a long career in aircraft design at Farnborough, in England, and the Aeronautical Research Laboratories in Melbourne.

Although I took up flying as a hobby in 1971 or 1972, my exposure to aircraft and aviation began in 1955 when, after leaving school one month after my sixteenth birthday, I commenced an electrical engineering cadetship, based at Launceston Airport, with the Department of Civil Aviation (DCA). At that time, the DCA was the federal body responsible for all airport operations and maintenance in the early days of air transportation in Australia. My work at Launceston Airport involved the installation and maintenance of the airport navigation aids, radio communications facilities, and runway lighting.

As well as being the commercial airport for the city of Launceston, Launceston Airport was a very popular light aircraft base, with the Launceston Aero Club using a grass strip parallel to the sealed runway. This was my first exposure to Tiger Moths, Auster, Stinson, and the early Cessna tail-dragger, the C170.

From this background, I developed the base knowledge and confidence that made me believe I could navigate my way around the world. Interestingly, however, this exposure to aircraft did not drive my passion for flying. It was more the technology of aircraft design and the electronic navigation equipment, coupled with the sense of accomplishment one gets from flying from point A to point B, that drove me to achieve the skill levels necessary to fly my family safely around the world.

Career Opportunity in the United States

In late 1963, at age twenty-five, I was a recently graduated, unmarried electrical engineer, working in Melbourne, Australia, for the Bureau of Meteorology on the design and production of recording weather stations using digital logic techniques. Computers then were in their infancy; they occupied entire glass-enclosed rooms and mostly used vacuum tubes as logic elements. Discrete transistors had only just hit the market, and it would be another six years before solid-state integrated circuits were introduced into the latest computers.

I was designing logic elements using the newly introduced solid-state transistors in early October 1963, when I attended a workshop in Melbourne, conducted by an American-based company, on the use of their new range of off-the-shelf logic modules for digital design. The workshop was led by Harlen Anderson, vice president and co-founder of Digital Equipment Corporation (DEC) of Maynard, Massachusetts, in the United States. By the end of the workshop, it was clear that using off-the-shelf logic elements was the way to go and that being involved in the evolution of digital design would be an exciting career direction.

I tracked Harlen down in his hotel and told him that I wanted to get together to discuss the possibility of my joining the company. I really knew little about the company, as it was, at that stage, still privately owned, but I was so excited by the concept and future of digital logic design for my career that I took this bold action, which was completely out of character with my normally conservative upbringing.

Harlen and I hit it off very well, and, after some discussion about Digital and its direction (founded in 1957, it had only just recently introduced its first computer to the market, the PDP1), he questioned me on my background and motivation. He made no commitment to me at that time, other than to say that he would discuss it with the company president, Ken Olsen, when he returned to the United States.

I had just about forgotten the meeting when, six weeks later, a letter arrived, making me an offer to join Digital in the United States for twelve months, to start in early January 1964. With a salary in American dollars, airfares and travel expenses provided, how could I refuse?

But there was a snag: I had been dating the entrancing Virginia Stabb in Melbourne for a couple of years. We had met at a dance when she was a sixteen-year-old high school student in Launceston, Tasmania, and she had just graduated as a nursing sister from the Royal Children's Hospital in Melbourne.

In the two months following the offer letter, Virginia and I decided to get married, arranged the wedding with both families in Hobart (Virginia's extended family lived there, and Virginia considered it her home town), got married on New Year's Day, 1964, and set off for a honeymoon in Hawaii on our way to Maynard where I would commence work with Digital on January 20.

This started a career trajectory for me that was inspirational. When I joined DEC, there were four hundred employees worldwide, and it grew at the rate of 30 per cent a year. When I quit in 1979, the company employed 83,000.

After twelve months in New England, in the United States, my career with Digital took me to Perth in Western Australia, in January 1965, for twelve months. There, I installed and maintained the main campus computer, a PDP6 time-sharing system (the first commercial time-sharing computer installation in the world). I went back to Sydney in January 1966 as founding managing director of the local Digital subsidiary. From 1966 to January 1970, I developed the company from just a secretary and myself to a staff of sixty-five with computer installations throughout Australia and New Zealand.

Meanwhile, on our family front, Angela was born in Perth on June 15, 1965; Stuart in Sydney on August 24, 1967; and Rowena in Sydney on January 21, 1970.

Shortly after Rowena's arrival, I was invited to return to the United States, this time in a market development role in Princeton, New Jersey, for twelve months. I was then promoted to global marketing manager for the soon-to-be-introduced PDP11/45–70 range of computers, which proved to be the main engine of growth for the company and was to the distributed processing segment of the computer industry what the IBM 360 was to the mainframe segment.

By late 1974, the PDP11/45 launch was a success, and the business had grown. DEC rewarded me with a range of stock options in the now publicly listed company Digital Equipment Corporation.

Now, Virginia and I faced a decision: whether to stay in the United States with our green cards for the secondary and tertiary phases of the children's education or to return to Sydney in time for the commencement of the 1976 school year.

We opted for Sydney. We also decided to fly home in our own aircraft.

The Decision

What led to the decision to fly our young family in a single-engine plane around the world?

Coming back to Australia was the same decision that many expatriates stationed overseas with young families eventually have to make. Should we settle for the long term overseas or return to the home country?

In late 1974, we were torn. I had a great opportunity to continue my career trajectory, and I needed to commit to a new role as a product manager and vice president within DEC immediately. Virginia and I both felt very strongly about a high-quality education for our children. Frankly, we did not feel we could give them the type of education we wanted in the United States. We wanted our children to have a Sydney-based private school education and to be educated as Australians.

So why not just book a commercial flight and fly back? Why take three months off and travel in a small plane halfway around the world?

For me, the question was largely, why not? I had challenged myself all the way through my career from small-town Tasmania to a global role. Right from the start of my career in IT, when I made the decision to accept Harlen's offer in Melbourne, I had not chosen the traditional route. As a result, I did not see any boundaries to many of my decisions. A trip around the world really just seemed like an extension to what we had already done – pack up the flying station wagon, kids, and gear and take the slightly longer flight legs than the ones we took in the United States.

Virginia embraced the idea of travelling around the world for an additional reason. Although she, in particular, placed a priority on giving her children an excellent education back in Australia, she was also focused on ensuring that our children were always open to new opportunities, like we had been. She felt that it was a great way to challenge the conservative influences of growing up in Massachusetts by giving the whole family an experience that would change their perspective forever.

And while we were both well aware of the amount of planning required to execute this type of trip and some of the risks, we remained, like everyone in the 1970s, optimistic about taking on a new challenge.

Gaining Wings

While living in Princeton in 1971, we occupied a small apartment on the outskirts, between Princeton and Trenton, New Jersey. One day, Virginia noticed an ad in the local Princeton rag for an evening course on the theory of private pilot flying, and, knowing my interest in flying, she suggested that I enrol. It was a six-month course, one night per week, and by the time I had completed the course and sat the exam, my job with Digital had taken us to Maynard, Massachusetts.

We moved into a small apartment in the town of Boxborough, a small town of twelve hundred people, forty-five minutes west of Boston, and a ten-minute drive to my office in the old mill in Maynard.

On the route between Maynard and Boxborough, we were fortunate to have a small light-aircraft airport called MinuteMan (MM) with a 2,800 ft. sealed runway, flight service facilities and a café, and, best of all, a flight instructor named Robert Wall.

Great! We wanted to give the children the opportunity to see more of the United States, and flight instruction at the time was relatively inexpensive.

Once we had settled into our accommodations and new job, I signed up with Robert for flight instruction, with the goal of obtaining my private pilot's license. My first supervised flight occurred on May 6, 1972, and I flew my first solo flight on June 17 after 14.8 hours of instruction. Advanced instruction continued with my first cross-country solo from MinuteMan to western Massachusetts on July 29 and the issuance of my private pilot's license on February 10, 1973, with a total flying time of 84.3 hours and pilot-in-command time (no other pilot or instructor on board) of 44.1 hours. This enabled me to fly under visual flight rules (VFR) conditions only, which meant I had to have more than three miles of visibility from the aircraft and to remain clear of clouds.

I began to feel more confident in my flying ability and started to take the family on short day trips in a four-seat Cessna 172. One of our favourite short trips was the forty-minute flight from MinuteMan to Martha's Vineyard and Nantucket Islands for the day. It would have taken most of the day just to get there by car and ferry, but with the aircraft, we were able to arrive by mid-morning, rent bicycles, sightsee around the island, have some lunch, do some more sightseeing, and then climb in the aircraft and be home by late afternoon.

It was this method of touring – flying to our destination then using bikes for local touring – that was to be our model for touring Europe.

Flying in All Weather Conditions

One trip north from MinuteMan with the family to the New Hampshire lakes area for the day caused me some doubts about my current level of proficiency for serious cross-country flying.

We departed MinuteMan in bright, clear early summer weather with a forecast for fine weather. After about an hour-and-a-half flying, however, the sky became very overcast, the cloud ceiling decreased to below 2000 ft., and it started to rain. To remain clear of clouds, I had to descend dangerously close to the ground in a very hilly area. That was enough for me. With the weather coming from the north, I turned 180 degrees and managed to stay clear of the worst of the weather and returned to MinuteMan.

This taught me that if I planned to venture more than fifty miles from our home airport, I needed to be able to fly and land in all forms of weather. To do this, I had to obtain an instrument rating on top of my private pilot's license, which would enable me to fly under instrument flight rules (IFR). IFR would enable me to fly with weather down to zero visibility en route and to make IFR approaches to airports with ground visibility down to one hundred meters.

In June 1973, I commenced a program to gain my first-class instrument rating, with initial blind flying in a simulator at Bedford airport, then instruction in an aircraft using a hood over my eyes that allowed me to see the instruments but prevented me from seeing outside the aircraft.

Six months of intensive training in all aspects of blind flying, including actual and hooded cross-country flights and instrument landings, gained me my instrument rating in late January 1974, with a total of 45.6 hours of instrument flying.

With some two hundred hours of flying experience and an instrument rating, I now felt much more confident about tackling the vagaries of the New England weather, from the visibility-reducing haze of summer to the fog, ice, and snow conditions of winter.

Experience in Higher-performance Aircraft

My early flight training was carried out in a small two-seat Cessna 150 trainer with a cruising speed of (105 kts, 190 kph) supplied by the flight school, then I graduated to the four-seat Cessna 172 (122 kts, 226 kph) for cross-country flights.

Both of these aircraft are very simple and forgiving high-wing monoplanes with fixed tricycle landing gear and fixed-pitch propellers. There isn't much to go wrong!

As my competency rose, and I started venturing from the home airport as pilot in command, load capacity (enough seating for Mum, Dad, and the three kids, plus luggage) became more important. Thumbing through a flying magazine one day, I saw an ad seeking partners in a syndicate of ten pilots to own and maintain a range of three aircraft based at Bedford airport, which was about thirty minutes from my home and fifteen minutes from my office. The syndicate was called Associated Pilots Inc. These are the three aircraft it owned:

Cessna 172 – fixed gear, fixed prop, 4 place, 122 kts (226 kph) cruising speed

Cessna 182 – fixed gear, variable pitch prop, 4 place, 135 kts (250 kph) cruising speed

Cessna 210 – retractable gear, variable pitch prop, 6 place, 170 kts (315 kph) cruising speed

This range was ideal for our needs, so I immediately invested and received instruction and checkout in all three aircraft by the group's flight instructor.

As a part-owner, my flying costs were now about half that of rental costs per hour, with only the fixed fees to cover the maintenance and depreciation, plus the variable fuel costs.

A considerable portion of my instrument instruction was carried out in the C182 and C210, as this was cheaper than renting a C172, and I gained valuable experience in the higher-performance aircraft. My first solo trip under instrument conditions was a business trip in the C182 to Cleveland, Ohio, via Buffalo, New York, and return, a total of eleven hours on an IFR flight plan.

My arrival at Buffalo was an ILS (instrument landing system) landing in low visibility, and much of the trip was VFR on top of cloud with descent through the cloud for landing. A commercial trip to the same destination would have required about the same time in the air, but with three separate legs each way via New York as the hub.

The Bahamas Trip

Building Experience over Water

By Christmas 1973, with low-cost access to a range of aircraft and a high level of competence under instrument conditions, the focus shifted over the next twelve months to family flying with trips to New York, via Teterboro Airport; Montreal, Canada; Princeton, New Jersey; Philadelphia, Pennsylvania; Norfolk, Virginia; and a great family holiday in 1974 to the Bahamas.

Winters in New England are very severe and long – with the first ice or snow typically in late October or early November and snow still on the ground up until April or May. The winter of 1973–74 was particularly severe, so in early April 1974, Virginia and I decided that a Bahamas holiday would thaw our frozen bodies. I had read in flying magazines of pilots hopping from island to island in their aircraft and sightseeing over the azure waters of the Caribbean.

This was for us!

With Bahamas Island VFR charts in my flight bag, backpacks with swimming and beach gear in the luggage bay, and a planned route from Boston, down the east coast, past New York, to West Palm Beach, Florida, the family and I boarded our trusty C210 and departed a cold and snowy Bedford airport on an IFR flight plan with a forecast of fine weather along the route. The estimated flight time to West Palm Beach was eight hours, with one re-fuelling stop.

An hour after departure, while crossing over the southern end of Connecticut in cloud at 7,000 ft., I noticed an ice build-up on the leading edge of the wings. Too much ice could distort the airflow over the wing and cause the plane to, literally, drop out of the sky.

Normally a change to a lower altitude and warmer air solves the problem, so I requested descent to 5,000 ft. from flight control, but this only seemed to make things worse, and a further descent to 3,000 ft. did not improve matters. With flight conditions rapidly deteriorating, our plight became quite serious. This was obviously noticed in my voice communications with flight control, when, without any further request from me, he suggested we divert to Long Island, and he would provide radar vectors for an ILS landing at Islip airport.

From the two front seats in the C210, the leading edge of the high-winged aircraft is clearly visible, so Virginia in the co-pilot's seat, for the first time in our flying together, became nervous as she observed the build-up of ice on the wing. Between the flight controller and Virginia, I got the message and turned left to follow his vectors to Islip. Virginia's confidence in me was restored.

As we moved towards the coast over Long Island, the air temperature at our flying altitude increased. The ice melted, and we were able to land at Islip without any further problems.

We took a room at a motel near the airport for the night and then we were on our way again in clear cloudless skies all the way down the coast to West Palm Beach, with a re-fuelling stop at Norfolk. Our flight path took us over the Verrazano Narrows Bridge, just to the east of Manhattan, so we had a spectacular view of the skyscrapers on Manhattan Island and the Statue of Liberty.

From West Palm Beach, we headed out over the water to Freeport on the Grand Bahama Island, then over the next ten days we went to Eleuthra, Exuma, and Nassau before heading back north to Boston with our great suntans.

The leg from West Palm Beach to Freeport, which was 100 miles (160 km), was my first extended over-water flight, and, as expected, I experienced a slight sensation of fear as we headed out over water for the first time with no land in sight.

The only incident we experienced on this trip was one that to this day has no rational explanation. The Bahamas are situated in an apex of a triangle defined by Bermuda, Puerto Rico, and the Bahamas. This triangle is known as the Bermuda Triangle, or Devil's Triangle, where some believe paranormal events occur in which the laws of physics do not apply. Though these occurrences remain an enigma, some kind of electromagnetic anomaly does occur in this region, which has affected ships and airplanes for centuries, often with disastrous consequences.

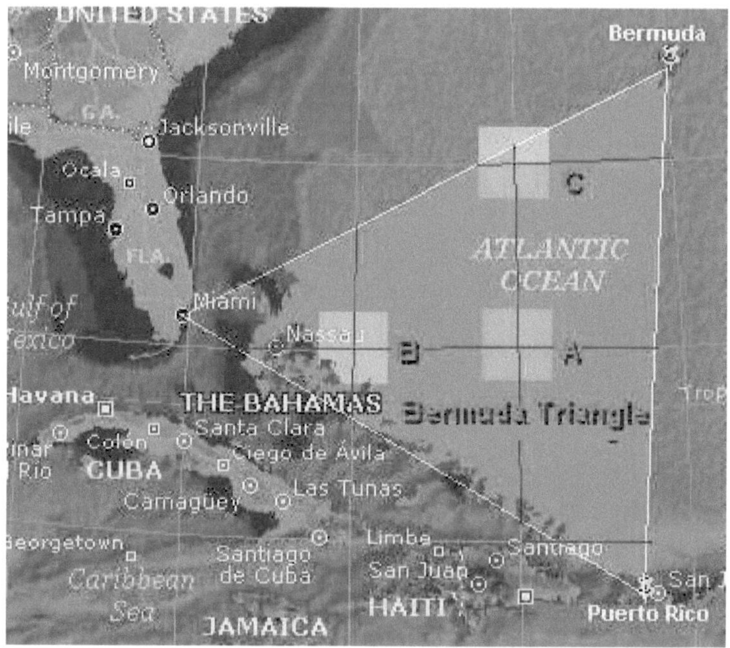

Figure 2 Bermuda or Devil's Triangle.

After no problems on our first leg in this area from West Palm Beach to Freeport, the next day we departed Freeport for North Eleuthra, a distance of about 160 miles (260 km).

With no en route VOR navigation in this area, rather than fly directly over water to North Eleuthra, I decided on a triangular route and flew along the coast of Grand Bahamas to Pelican Point on the eastern tip, then I set a compass heading over the water that would take us past the southern tip of Great Abaco Island to the northern tip of Eleuthra.

Over the top of the eastern tip of Great Bahamas, I set my compass heading for Eleuthra and verified this with a radio bearing on my automatic direction finder (ADF) from a commercial radio station at Pelican Point. Half an hour into the leg, when I should have had Great Abaco Island in sight, there was nothing but water! After another fifteen minutes, when I should have been at my destination, there was still no land in sight. So I promptly did a 180-degree turn and retraced my route to Grand Bahama, using the ADF as my radio compass.

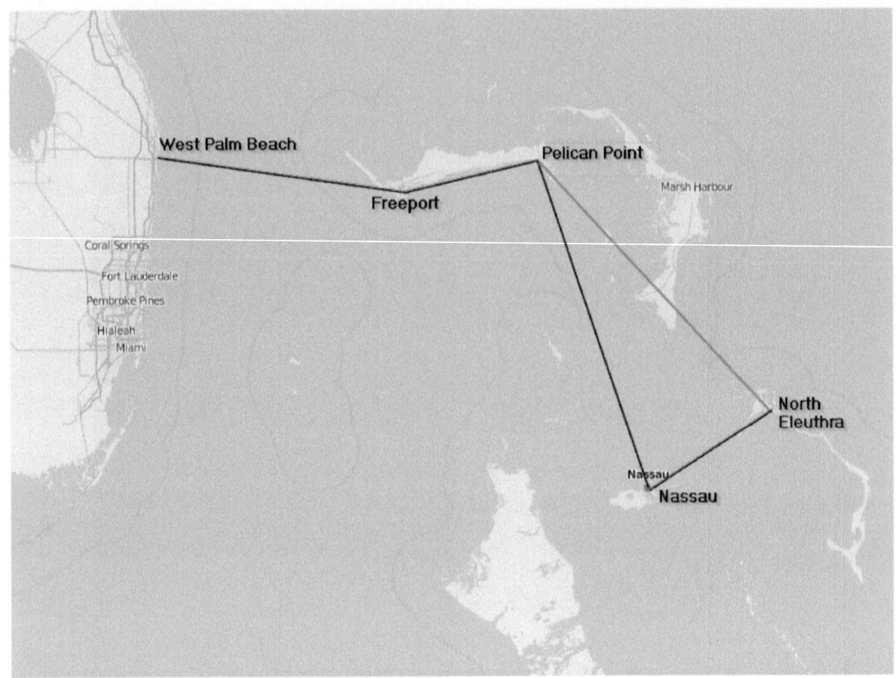

Figure 3 Devil's Triangle with my original course (light grey) and revised course (black).

For this sort of navigation error to have occurred over such a short distance, the compass had to have been in error by at least 20–30 degrees. I could not understand it, but, rather than repeat the error, I reset our course to fly via the capital of the Bahamas, Nassau, which has a VOR beacon. We were then able to fly along an in-bound VOR radial to Nassau, then an outbound radial that took us directly to the airport at North Eleuthra. No wonder so many aircraft and ships have been lost in the Devil's triangle, particularly in the days before radio and GPS navigation.

Figure 4 Approaching North Eleuthra from the air.

The rest of our Bahamas trip proceeded uneventfully, with four days of sun, sand, and clear blue water at each of Eleuthra and Exuma Islands and two days duty-free shopping at Nassau, before we headed back up the coast to Bedford via Norfolk.

Apart from the spectacular ocean vistas over the Bahamas, the most amazing site en route was when we passed over the Kennedy (Cape Canaveral) Spaceport, where a large Atlas rocket was on the pad, ready for launching.

Virginia's Perspective on the Bahamas Trip

Virginia had her own unique perspective on this trip, which she wrote in her diary:

> The Bahamas lie approximately 6 3/4 flying hours south of Massachusetts and one hour west of West Palm Beach, Florida. The climate is tropical, the islands sparsely populated, and the people happy natured and seeming to be in no hurry. We took food with us and also life-preserving equipment for the inter-island flights. Our route was as follows:
>
> Massachusetts, West Palm Beach (two overnight stops), Freeport, Grand Bahama Island (one night), Spanish Wells via

North Eleuthra (four nights), Georgetown, Exuma (four nights), Nassau, Paradise Island (two nights), Norfolk, Virginia, via West Palm Beach (one night) back to Massachusetts. Phew!

Robin's plane is a six-seat Cessna 210 (with one seat removed) and has plenty of room for us all and such souvenirs as some pieces of coral rock, lots of unusual pods found in Nassau, and a soda bottle full of Bahamas sand.

The flight right down the east coast of the USA was spectacular. Robin flew at 7,000 ft. by IFR flight plan in clear VFR conditions, so we usually had a good view of what was going on underneath. I just didn't know that America was a land of such contrasts. We skirted New York City – the skyscrapers looked like great fingers arising from Manhattan whilst all the buildings on the surrounding countryside were of normal size. We then flew down Chesapeake Bay and picked out the island of Tangier that we had read about in a recent National *Geographic* magazine. As we flew over Norfolk, Virginia (we stayed there on our return journey), we saw part of a large fleet of U.S. Navy vessels 'in mothballs'. Stuart was ecstatic when he looked down on all of this. As we flew over Virginia and the Carolinas, most of the country below us was cultivated in large areas or used for grazing cattle, very different from the small farms that one sees in Massachusetts.

By now the children were not too interested in the countryside below us; they had been in the air for four hours and were in need of a stretch. They were cranky and irritable. All this changed as we sped southward and Robin pointed out to us all Cape Canaveral and the large blockhouse in the centre of it all where those exciting space flights were launched.

After this, we followed Florida's marvellous beaches, inland waterways, and citrus groves southward, until, at 4.30 p.m., we landed at West Palm Beach. Our hotel here backed onto a golf course where major tournaments are held, and just about everything seemed green and fringed with hibiscus blooms, a welcome sight after the long northern winter.

I absolutely believe in Robin's capability as a pilot; he has just the right mixture of aggressiveness and caution in his make-up. But the following day, as we flew from Freeport out over the water to North Eleuthra, I found out quickly what fear is. As the airplane gained height, the horizon disappeared completely and sea was joined to sky. The reason for this is that the water is warmed by a current and when the cooler air meets it a mist is formed. So here we were flying through blue nothingness, and I thank heaven for modern radio, navigational aids, and Robin's ability to use them.

Commercial License

This trip to the Bahamas convinced me that I should improve my flying skills with more instruction, so I decided to raise my proficiency with instruction leading to the awarding of a commercial pilot's license.

The program commenced late September 1974 and involved precision flying of the larger aircraft (C210, C182, C206), both in visual and instrument conditions, including aerobatics, spins, spirals, precision landings, and other manoeuvres.

After about fifty hours of solo flying practice and instruction, I was awarded my commercial license at the end of June 1975, shortly before we planned to depart for our trip home.

Planning

Having made the decision to return to Australia in our own aircraft, and with about eight months to scheduled departure, Virginia and I had a lot of planning to do for the trip from Boston to Sydney, with some touring around Europe on the way.

- We needed to plan the route with geo-political, fuel range, and aircraft loading considerations in mind.
- Virginia has charge of the touring route and stops around Europe.
- We needed to select a suitable aircraft and its navigation and communications capabilities and place an order and schedule delivery with enough time before departure to shake down any production bugs in the new aircraft, and in the pilot as well.
- With the plan to sell the aircraft in our destination country, Australia, we had to be sure that it met Australian registration requirements.

And we did all this while trying to manage a young family and hold down a very challenging job right up to the day of departure.

Which Route?

The decision about which route to take was easy. We could travel west or east. West would take us from Boston via California, Hawaii, and Fiji to Sydney. East would take us from Boston via Canada, Greenland, Iceland, Europe, the Middle East, and through South-east Asia to Australia.

With the family on board, there was really only one choice, east, because of the extensive over-water legs of the west-bound route. We would need a Cessna business jet for that; our budget would allow only a single-engine piston aircraft, and with five people plus luggage on board, perhaps a six-seater.

Which Aircraft?

The choices boiled down to the Cessna 210; the Cessna 206, a station-wagon version of the C210 with the same engine but with fixed gear and double loading doors at the rear; the Beechcraft A36 with a low wing, retractable gear, and double loading doors; or the Piper Cherokee 6, with fixed gear and low wing.

While we would have liked a top-of-the-line Beechcraft (the Mercedes of the air!), the budget and payload narrowed the choices down to one, the Cessna 206 Stationair with its higher payload, fixed gear (less to go wrong), and more spacious cabin and luggage space than the C210 or the Cherokee 6. In the C206 we traded off speed for carrying capacity, and it was considerably cheaper.

How Much Fuel?

The C206 has a cruising speed of 142 kts (280 kph) versus a C210 at 170 kts (315 kph). A detailed analysis of our route showed that at cruising speed we would require enough fuel on-board for the longest leg over water from Iceland to Ireland (eight hours without reserves), but for the rest of the trip, six hours plus reserves would be the maximum required.

As the standard 206 aircraft had a maximum range of six hours, including reserves, we would need booster tanks located in the cabin with a pump up to the high-mounted wing tanks. Make that two tanks: one to meet the needs of the Iceland–Ireland leg, 100 US gallons (378 litres) for a total of thirteen hours with comfortable reserves, and one for the rest of the trip, 30 U.S. gallons (114 litres) for a total of eight hours with comfortable reserves, but only one connected into the fuel system at a time.

We had previously decided that I should be accompanied by a fellow pilot for the long Atlantic crossing, and the family would fly commercial to Ireland. This meant that the aircraft would be configured with two seats, the one hundred–gallon tank occupying the floor-to-ceiling space of the next row of seats, and the spare tank and luggage, including bikes, on the third row of seats and in the luggage bay.

For the rest of the trip, we would re-configure the aircraft in Ireland, replacing the one hundred–gallon tank with a thirty-gallon tank that would occupy the floor space of one seat, install the additional three seats for the passengers, and stow the bikes and luggage in the bay behind the rear seats.

For the Atlantic crossing with full fuel, seats, luggage, and bikes, we calculated that the aircraft would be 300 lbs (136 kg) over its nominal gross weight. This would require special approval to be obtained by Wiggins Airways in Norward, Massachusetts, which was the company installing the tanks.

When the one hundred–gallon tank was removed in Ireland, the gross weight with full fuel and our three light passengers would be reduced to the normal 3,600 lbs (1,633 kg), with a maximum endurance of eight hours, a good margin for safety on this trip.

What Radio Communications Gear?

In North America and Europe, the only requirement for radio voice communications is a VHF transmitter/receiver, which provides line-of-sight communications (greater than two hundred miles at normal cruising altitudes) between ground control and all aircraft, including other commercial aircraft.

The Australian registration of aircraft then required ground-to-ground (non-line-of-sight) communications over vast distances on the Australian continent, which in turn requires a high-frequency (HF) transmitter/receiver. HF transmission works by bouncing the radio wave on the underside of the stratosphere back to earth, so transmissions can be received from any location on earth to any other location. As we planned to register and then re-sell the aircraft in Australia, we decided to order the machine with the HF transceiver installed from Cessna, allowing us to have the use of it in emergencies on our trip.

Where to Place the Order?

When it came time to obtain a quote for the specific aircraft and configuration, we appeared to have two choices: order an Australian-registered C206 through the Australian agent Rex Aviation or order a US-registered C206 with specific factory modifications to meet Australian registration requirements, including the HF radio.

We asked for a quote from Rex with the Australian agent's mark-up, but the Australian air attaché in Washington informed me that I would be unable to fly an Australian-registered aircraft with a US pilot's license. Worse, there was no way I could obtain an Australian license before reaching Australia. So I called the local Cessna representative, Ted

Keen of Door Aviation, and he supplied a very favourable quote for the aircraft. However, soon after we placed the order, Cessna said that some of the equipment ordered on my aircraft was available only to aircraft destined for export and not available to their Massachusetts representative. I called the head of Cessna marketing and explained what we planned to do, including the flight to Australia. This raised his level of interest as I am sure he saw the potential for publicity from the sale.

In retrospect, I should have taken the opportunity of seeking sponsorship from the supplier for the adventure, but in those days sponsorship was not as popular as it is today.

When he realized what we were doing, he had a talk with manufacturing and accepted the order for the Australian-specified aircraft for domestic US delivery.

The two important items in the aircraft required for Australian conditions were the specific Australian seatbelts needed for the two front seats and a HF radio receiver/transmitter necessary for long-distance communications in the remote parts of the world to which we were destined to travel.

Apparently HF radios are not used in North America at all and were, therefore, unfamiliar to the local Cessna people. We placed the order in mid-February; they quoted delivery for the end of May. If they were on time, it would allow two month's shakedown of the aircraft before our planned departure date of August 1.

My previous experience with Cessna avionics had been a dismal failure, and so I did not order any of Cessna's radio gear with the aircraft. I planned to have a complete set of King avionics installed by a local radio shop in New England. I had been very impressed with the quality and reliability of the King equipment installed in the Cessna 210 of Associated Pilots Inc.

Flight Preparation

Fortunately, most countries do not require any flight approval for aircraft registered in countries that are members of the International Civil Aviation Organisation. Approval is implicit with the filing and approval of a flight plan from an airport in one country to the airport of entry in another country.

The source of all this information was a very helpful book published by the US Government called the *International Flight Information*

Manual, which lists by country the flight approval, visa requirements, and airports of entry. It is published principally for military air force personnel flying aircraft around the world, but it applied equally to civilian personnel as long as the aircraft was of US registry and the crews were US citizens. All international aircraft must enter and leave from airports of entry when flying into or out of the country. This information, of course, was essential for us in planning our route. Ahmadabad in India, for example, was not a place we would have chosen to stop, but it was the first airport of entry into India from Pakistan.

The US Government, through its Defence Mapping Agency, was also the source of the World Aeronautical Charts (WAC) for operational navigation needed for VFR flying for the complete route from Boston to Sydney.

Slowly we built up more and more information about all aspects of our trip, and, as we did so, our confidence continued to build. We were rapidly approaching the point of no return: the point at which we could cancel the order for the aircraft and proceed home by commercial airlines as any sane family would do.

Someone Else Has Done It!

During the negotiations for the purchase of the aircraft with Ted Keen, he said that nine months earlier he had sold a new Cessna 182 to a consulting engineer in Boston who had then flown that aircraft along the same route to Australia. This really excited us, especially as Ted was able to give us the name and address of the pilot who had made the trip. I rushed to the phone almost immediately and called him.

The man, Alve Ericsson, was only too happy to get together, and we arranged to meet at a restaurant in Cambridge to spend the night talking about his experiences and our plans. We had a very pleasant dinner and discussion, and both Virginia and I came away from that meeting with our confidence boosted tremendously by both the experiences he had shared and the advice he had to offer concerning the trip.

Alve, it seemed, had made the trip all the way from Boston to Sydney in six weeks and was alone for most of the trip. He had built a very large gas storage capacity inside the aircraft and was able to fly up to sixteen hours non-stop with normal reserves at the end of that time.

The route he had taken was almost identical to our own plans, with the exception that he flew non-stop from Gander, Newfoundland, to

Reykjavik, Iceland, and with his larger tanks was able to fly non-stop from Bali, Indonesia, to Darwin.

The only delay that Alve had experienced during the whole trip was on the Indonesian section of the journey when he was held up in Singapore for three weeks as he waited for flight approval to overfly Indonesia. We had reason to heed his advice on how to minimize this delay, and, despite all precautions, we too were held up in Singapore for a week on our journey.

Because of Alve's warnings, we wrote immediately to the Indonesian consulate in New York and to the US embassy in Jakarta. We requested details of the procedure to be followed to obtain flight approval to land in Indonesia. The Indonesian consulate was very helpful in providing a list of the addresses and telephone numbers of the Australian, US, and Indonesian consulates in Singapore and the Australian embassy in Jakarta but said that any flight approval would have to be applied for at the US embassy in Jakarta.

However, the US embassy in Jakarta said they could not help us directly with flight approval, instead giving us a list of three agents residing in Jakarta who could obtain the flight approval for us. We immediately cabled one of the agents but did not receive his response until just before we departed in July (he had sent his letter by surface mail, which took about two months from Jakarta). He said he required a fee of about US$60 and requested full details of our planned itinerary through Indonesia. He also said he needed two months to obtain flight approval, so we responded immediately with the $60 and full details of our planned itinerary in Indonesia.

By the time any response could have been received from him, we had already flown out of the United States. We just had to cross our fingers and hope that the approval was waiting for us by the time we arrived in Singapore. The only other country which was difficult to obtain flight approval for was Burma, and we immediately wrote to the Burmese consulate in New York to request their procedure for obtaining flight approval. We received immediate acknowledgment from New York that the matter had been referred to the civil aviation authorities in Rangoon; however, no more was heard from the Rangoon authorities before our departure.

No Turning Back

By the end of April, we were virtually committed to go. I notified my employer that I intended to make the trip and requested an extended vacation of three months so that we would not feel rushed at all on the journey.

Bicycles were to be our vital means of ground travel between the airport and points of interest in Europe, and Virginia and the kids set out to select the best bikes for the job. They chose a beautiful set of English Raleigh touring bicycles with three-speed gears. They were ideal for stowing in the aircraft as they folded up. The same sized bicycle could be used by all the family, from eight-year-old Stuart to me, because the bikes were equipped with extra-long adjustable columns on both the seat and handle bars. To accommodate Rowena, who was five, we bought a plastic carrying seat to mount on the rear of my bike. In hindsight, she was a little large for the seat, but she enjoyed the ride and was able to participate in all the activities with the rest of the family.

The Australian consulate in New York provided visa requirements for all the countries we planned to visit. There were only three countries that required prior visa approval: Iran, Burma, and Indonesia. Because it would be about three months before we entered those countries, we were unable to obtain visas before leaving Boston: the maximum length of visa approval was three months.

Aircraft Delivery and Ferry Flight

By the first of June, two months before our scheduled departure, the aircraft was due for delivery, so I placed an order at a local aircraft radio installation shop to install the King radio and navigation equipment. The whole family was eagerly awaiting the trip, and the next two months were among the most hectic we have ever experienced.

I had arranged to take personal delivery of the aircraft in Wichita, and, as it would not be equipped with any navigation or communication radios on delivery, I would borrow from the radio shop a portable communication and navigation set to install before the first flight.

On the morning of Friday, June 13, our agent said the aircraft was ready. I couldn't wait, so that afternoon I took a commercial aircraft out of Boston for Wichita, arrived late that night, and settled into my hotel in a pitch of excitement. Tomorrow I would take delivery of my first aircraft!

The Midwestern sun was up bright and early and so was I, for breakfast and a cab directly to the Cessna delivery centre in South Wichita. They finalized the pre-delivery, then the 206 was taxied around in front of the terminal. I recognized it immediately. It had a great colour combination: white with red and brown stripes.

I was about to sign for the aircraft when they told me that, only the week before, the 206 had been left outside in a very violent hailstorm. Sigh. I inspected the aircraft but could not distinguish any form of damage at all. Generously, the Cessna people pointed out a couple of very small dents in the skin of the aircraft and allowed me a credit of $400 on the price.

Halfway across America on Compass and Clock

My first tasks were to install the small VHF antenna in the belly of the fuselage, connect the VHF communications set, and check out the communications with the local tower. The Cessna airport did not have a VOR, so there was no way I could check the portable VOR set that I had on board. Communications checked out well, and I was ready to taxi and depart for the first flight in my Cessna 206.

Actually, this was to be my first flight in any Cessna 206, but because it was very similar to the Cessna 210 in which I'd had some 150 hours flying time, I felt at home getting in behind the controls.

Taxiing out towards the departure end of the airport, I took it very slowly indeed, getting the feel of the aircraft and treating it very carefully. It had only had 2.5 hours of actual flying time, and it was a brand-new aircraft.

With departure clearance from the tower, I selected ten degrees of flaps, turned onto the runway, and pushed down the throttle for maximum take-off power. We – the aircraft and I – were in the air quickly, and, as I climbed 150 ft., the aircraft felt very comfortable. I had the feeling that I knew what to expect from it at all times.

Once clear of the Cessna control area, I set the compass heading on north-east and tried tuning in the Wichita VOR. To my dismay, there was no indication on the VOR at all, so I was left with no navigation equipment apart from compass and clock, not even an ADF.

Luckily, the weather out of Wichita was fine and clear, but, as I approached Chicago, the weather worsened, and on the horizon, over the nose, I could see great towering cumulonimbus clouds, indicating a line of thunderstorms just west that was moving south-east.

To circle around this line of thunderstorms, I turned due east, but, after another one hundred miles, I realized I had not reached the end of the line of storms and was forced to turn farther south to escape them.

At this stage, with visibility lowering to less than three miles, my navigation was limited to visual contact with railroad tracks and highways (IFR – I follow roads).

In the Midwest, all local roads line up either in a north–south or east–west direction, so it was comparatively easy to follow the roads and identify major highways as they cut across this pattern. At all times, I felt I had a clear path to the south to escape the bad weather if the visibility continued to deteriorate in the direction of my heading.

With low visibility over Madison, Indiana, there suddenly loomed another thunderstorm with lightning arcing from the base of the cumulonimbus cloud to the ground. I turned due south only to find, after ten minutes, another thunderstorm blocking my path. I was now down to 1,000 ft. above the ground and appeared to have thunderstorms all around me. Just as I started to look for a place to put the aircraft down, I noticed a bright patch of sunlight in the south-east and made a break for it.

Once through the gap, I was able to read the name of a small town on the local water tank and, hence, was able to pinpoint my position accurately by reference to the chart in my lap. I made track directly for the nearest large airport with a flight service facility, which was Lexington, Kentucky. There I checked the radar reports and found that the squall line was about thirty miles from the airport and closing in rapidly. Oh, how I wished I'd had my normal communications and navigation equipment on board.

I realized then how spoilt I had been, as the method I was using at this time was the same used in the pioneering days of aircraft flying in the early 1900s.

Now that I was in front of the storm line, I was determined to outrun it and set off immediately for the next point of destination where I planned to stop overnight: Columbus, Ohio. Next morning, the weather was clear, but a check with the forecaster indicated that weather over the Great Lakes and northern New York State would be cloudy and foggy, with low visibility in haze. Out of Columbus, I headed due north to hit Lake Erie, then I followed the shoreline of Lake Erie north-east to Buffalo.

Approaching Buffalo, the weather continued to deteriorate, but by flying about 2,000 ft. I was able to pick up the New York freeway and follow it to my next re-fuelling point, Syracuse. From there, I flew along the freeway to Albany, where the weather was very poor and visibility below VFR minimums. However, with the aid of Albany radar and a friendly operator, I made a radar approach. After two hours' delay, waiting for the fog and haze to lift at Albany, I decided that the weather had improved enough to enable me to follow the New York freeway south to pick up the Massachusetts Turnpike and follow it in through the Berkshire Hills and eastwards towards Boston.

At Rt. 495, I turned to the north and finally reached MinuteMan about 2.30 p.m. on Sunday, touching down on the 2,800-ft. strip. After twelve-and-a-half hours of some of the most difficult flying I had ever done, halfway across America, I had landed only two miles from our house in Boxborough.

I phoned the family, and they rushed over to inspect our new toy. Not wasting time, later that afternoon, I departed for Manchester, New Hampshire, the home base of Ed Stead, who was to install all the communications and navigation equipment. Virginia then drove from Boxborough to Manchester to bring me back home after what had been a very eventful two days.

Aircraft Shakedown and Familiarization

When the aircraft was returned to MinuteMan, on June 24, after the communications and navigation equipment were installed, it still had only 14.75 hours on the clock (approximately 4,000 km), and the family had not yet had a flight.

There were only six weeks to go before our scheduled departure, so we embarked on a series of cross-country flights to shake out any problems in the aircraft and to become thoroughly familiar with its systems and instruments.

My flight log showed we did six hours of actual and simulated instrument flying and approaches: a trip to Nantucket Island with family and bikes on board for the day; a 3.2-hour overnight trip with family and bikes to visit friends in northern Maine; a 4-hour dead-reckoning exercise (compass and stopwatch only) with my intended co-pilot, Tom Stockebrand, from MinuteMan to Providence, Rhode Island, and Hartford, Connecticut, and return; and a 2.5-hour dummy run with Tom up the coast of Maine to New Brunswick, Canada, and return with the long-distance tanks installed.

So after a month, by July 25, the aircraft had 48.2 hours on the clock, without any sign of a fault. We were feeling very confident with our aircraft and found it a delight to fly even when fully loaded.

Final preparations involved an annual inspection that day (not needed but carried out as a precaution), the installation of the big one hundred–gallon tank in the cabin, and a final radio check and a swinging of the magnetic compass, as the steel tank had changed the calibration.

On July 30, the aircraft was ready, and we spent the day re-configuring the cabin for the North Atlantic crossing with bikes, life raft, life jackets, EPIRB, and wetsuits on board and seats stowed.

Departure Boston – Destination Sydney

The North Atlantic Leg

The Canadian tundra is a very desolate rocky area, and, as we scooted across the sky, I wondered at the skills and understanding of the bush pilots who fly in this remote area of Northern Canada. Just three-and-a-half hours out from Moncton, we made first contact with the Goose Bay VOR and also the Goose Bay area controller.

Weather conditions at Goose Bay were overcast at 3,000 ft., so we appeared to have good conditions for landing. Local radar picked us up when we were still twenty miles out and provided vectors for a ground control approach (GCA). Having only previously done one GCA approach, this was good practice, and the approach controller talked us down to within 50 ft. of the runway, at which stage I took over and landed visually.

As Goose Bay is primarily a military airport, the GCA controller also welcomed the opportunity to practice his skills. After taxiing to the airport apron, we re-fuelled and parked the 206 and then checked in to the local hostel accommodation.

The route chosen for our North Atlantic crossing – Goose Bay, in northern Canada, to Narsarsuaq, Greenland, to Reykjavik, Iceland, and then to Shannon, Ireland, was what was known during World War II as the 'Snowball Route'. This route was used during the war to ferry fighter and bomber aircraft manufactured in Canada and America to the European theatre of operations.

Due to wartime urgency, Goose Bay was constructed in seventy-nine days, in 1941, with the completion of three 7,000-ft. runways. This facility was subsequently leased to the US government as a strategic American air force base.

On the Snowball Route, Narsarsuaq was known as Bluie West 1.

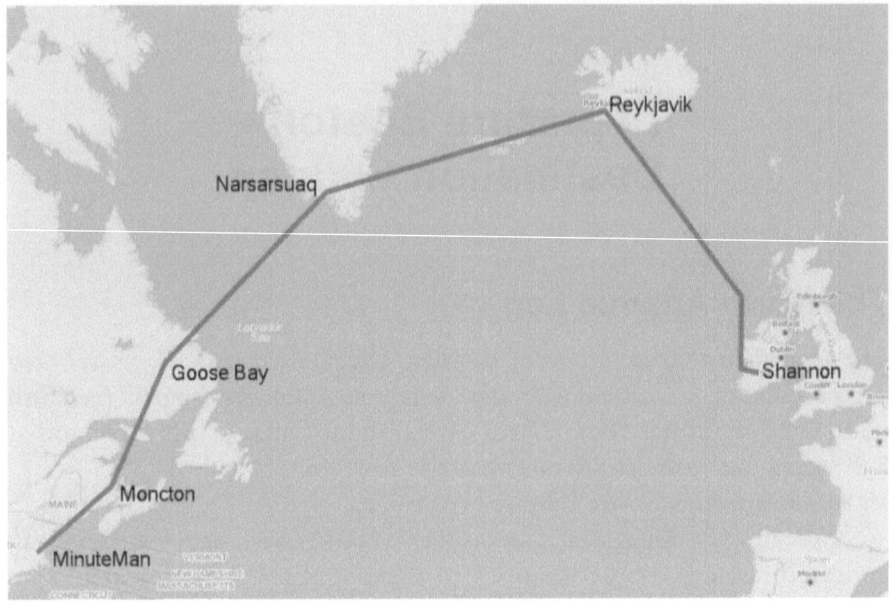

Figure 5 Our route from MinuteMan to Shannon.

Tom and I had allowed ourselves a week to cross the North Atlantic, so we settled in to wait for ideal weather for the crossing, not just for the first leg but a forecast of fine weather for the next three days, enough time for us to reach Shannon, Ireland.

Weather forecasting facilities at Goose Bay were very good as they serviced both military and civilian needs. We were handed a set of radar weather reports each morning for all altitude levels to 40,000 ft. and also forecasts for the next three days, including forecast winds *aloft*[x].

Forecast wind direction and strength at our flying altitudes was very important: the only means of navigation across the North Atlantic was dead reckoning with compass and clock, with the exception of the radio beacons for one hundred miles at each end of a leg.

After arriving on the evening of August 1 in Goose Bay, because of inclement weather, we had to wait until the evening of August 3 before we could schedule an early morning departure for Monday, the fourth.

That morning was bright and clear as we walked to the flight briefing room to file our flight plan to Reykjavik via Narsarsuaq.

Tom recalls:

In the briefing room we met a sixty-five-year-old lady who routinely ferries single-engine Beechcraft Bonanza aircraft non-stop across the

Atlantic directly from Goose Bay to Shannon in Ireland. She said two things I remember:

1. To do this crossing you don't need to be courageous, just optimistic.
2. Remember the frequency, 206 kHz. It is a pirate radio broadcast station off the coast of Iceland, which is much stronger (and hence has a greater range) than the other NDB navigation stations in the North Atlantic, and it's located where you want to go.

   This was good advice in case we missed the much shorter range NAV Aids.

After filing our flight plan, Tom and I loaded some snack food on board and started the engine for departure from Goose Bay to Narsarsuaq, near the southern tip of Greenland.

On climb out from Goose Bay, we were able to set our magnetic compass heading to Narsarsuaq, allowing for the local magnetic deviation of twenty-seven degrees west and the forecast wind at our cruising altitude of 7,000 ft., and to check this heading for one hundred miles from departure using the direction of the Goose Bay itself as the guide as it pointed directly towards our destination

The closer you are to the North Pole, the greater the deviation between true north and magnetic north. When flying in a generally easterly direction, this variable deviation needs to be applied to your compass heading to follow the plotted course over the water.

After flying for forty-five minutes, we were out over the ocean, which left us with three hours' dead-reckoning navigation and no radio voice communications over the North Atlantic before expecting to sight the Greenland ice cap off the nose of the aircraft.

But just two hours of smooth flying and clear conditions later, Tom noticed fuel leaking from the overflow pipe in the wing tank on the passenger's side of the aircraft and the wing skin ballooning. The wing tanks are constructed with a rubber bladder inside the wing structure, which, under pressure, inflated the skin.

Tom was clearly very disturbed, and I must admit I also felt a sense of panic. Alone in a small, single-engine aircraft over the North Atlantic Ocean with icebergs floating below and more than two hundred miles from land, the options for survival were very limited if the engine failed because of poor fuel management.

After the initial panic, and a few cross words between the two of us, our engineering logic came to our rescue, and we worked out that we had the fuel tank selector in the wrong position so that fuel was being pumped from the large cabin tank into the wing tank instead of directly into the engine, causing a build-up of pressure in the tank and an overflow of fuel.

Moving the selector to the correct position allowed the wing to revert to its normal shape and for Tom and me to resume normal breathing!

Several months after this trip, when I returned to Massachusetts for a visit, I learned that the only aspect of our Atlantic crossing Tom recounted to his friends was the fuel tank episode!

Three-and-a-half hours into the flight, and right on time, the ADF picked up the radio beacon at Julianefab, the entrance to the fjord leading to Narsarsuaq, and the needle pointed dead ahead, indicating we were right on course.

Tom Remembers:

As we approached Greenland, we could see what looked like a cloud bank on the horizon, but it never seemed to get any closer, even after another hour of flying. Turns out, it was the sheer edge of the Greenland ice cap with the 12,000-ft. plateau of ice behind it.

Closer to the coast, a field of small icebergs passed beneath our aircraft. The icebergs looked like little grains shaken out of a salt shaker on the black surface of the sea. On closer inspection, each tiny white dot had a ring of blue around it – the undersea 90 per cent of the 'berg.

Reaching the coast of Greenland and positively identifying the entrance to the Tungdliarfik Fjord that led to the airport at Narsarsuaq, one hundred miles inland, was not the last of our navigation worries on this leg.

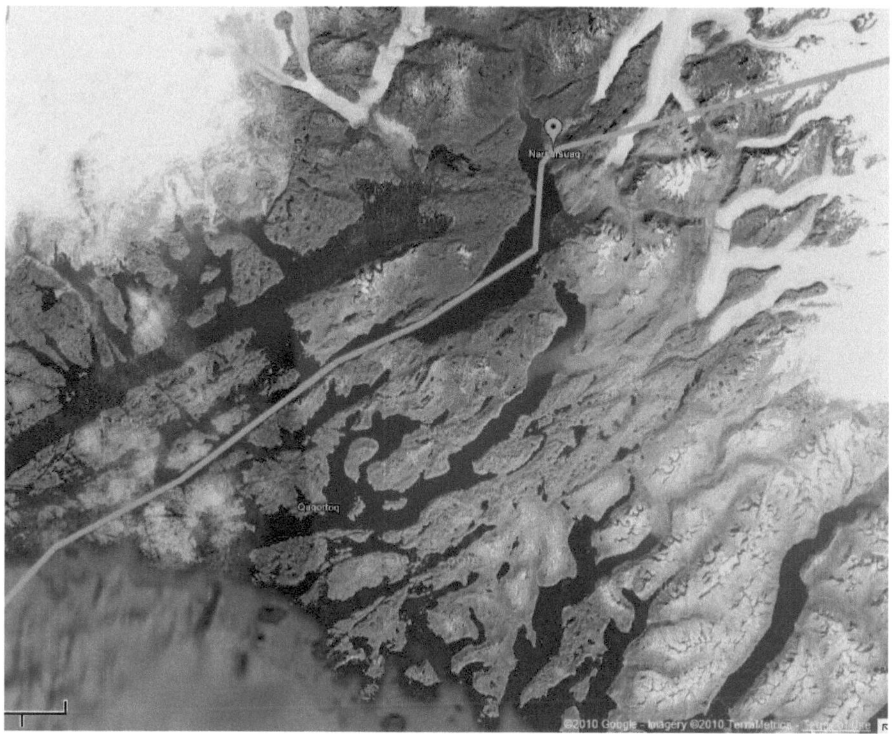

Figure 6 Flying up the Tungdliarfik Fjord.

As can be seen from the satellite photo, the fjord is as narrow as 1-km wide in places with walls rising to 5,000 ft. Dead-end branches led off the main passageway, so, with little room to manoeuvre, it was critical that we identify the correct course to follow on our maps as the cloud base was below the tops of the surrounding terrain.

After about an hour's flying up the fjord and a sharp left turn, the airport runway came into view.

Carved into the base of a mountain, the short, one-way runway extends uphill from the water's edge towards the 5,000-ft. mountain with the ice cap rising up behind it.

Figure 7 On final, Narsarsuaq.

Narsarsuaq was only scheduled to be a re-fuelling stop, so, while the tanks were being refilled, Tom and I surveyed this famous wartime landing strip and looked in awe at the ice cap extending from sea level to over 12,000 ft. within ten miles from the airport. Our route would take us up and over this ice cap on our easterly heading to Reykjavik, Iceland.

Tom recalls:

When we enquired about food, we were directed to an ugly blue World War 2 concrete block building for lunch. We expected burnt hamburgers, but, when we got inside there was a wonderful full Danish smorgasbord laid out in an elegant setting, complete with caviar, pickled herring, and the works. Apparently, this was the fare served up to the tourist boats that regularly visit this area.

We still had plenty of daylight available, and the weather remained fine, so we did not waste much time in getting airborne again and tackling the steep climb up over the ice cap. We knew that with full fuel and a gross weight 300 lbs over the maximum, we had a maximum ceiling of 13,000 ft., or no more than 1,000 ft. over the top of the ice cap.

We set full power and the propeller on fine pitch (equivalent to low gear in a car) and spiralled up directly over the airport to 13,000 ft. before setting course for Iceland. There was a white cloud base at 15,000 ft. and white ice cap below at 12,000 ft. The aircraft was on the upper limit of its flying capabilities, and we were under virtual IFR conditions with no horizon for two hundred miles before we cleared the east coast of Greenland and headed out over the ocean.

Prior to our departure, we had heard tales of aircraft flying in these white-on-white conditions and crashing on the ice cap when their pilots became disoriented. My instrument flying capabilities and careful observation of shadows on the snow surface helped to ensure we did not meet the same fate.

It was dead-reckoning navigation again, but with the added benefit of a VOR beacon within two hundred miles reception at our destination, so we had far more margin for error than on the previous leg, despite an estimated flying time of seven hours.

Tom remembers:

We had worked out the course across Greenland carefully but were off about ten degrees as we passed the east coast. Robin noticed this by checking landmarks on the coast and was able to correct the heading before we left land. This was a good thing because, over the long distance to Iceland, a ten-degree error would have had us pass well to the south of Iceland and over the North Sea before we struck more land. I don't know whether it was my error, unforeseen change in wind direction, or what!

The weather remained fine and clear on this leg, and, after five-and-a-half hours without any discernable landmark, what a relief it was when the VOR needle started to show signs of life. We were able to home in on this to Reykjavik and landed late Monday evening (Reykjavik time) after eleven hours flying for the day in mostly benign weather.

Tom recalls:

The hourly position reports we sent via our HF radio were completely guesswork. Indeed, we were an hour late at Reykjavik due to head winds, but the customs lady waited in her car till we did get in around midnight.

We checked into a hotel close to the airport, and then Tom and I obtained the forecast from flight service, determining that the next day (Tuesday) would not be the best for the long flight to Ireland, especially after just completing eleven hours in the pilot's seat.

The forecast for Wednesday was much brighter, so we opted for a lay-day, called Virginia and the kids at Audrey's place in Massachusetts (our friends Audrey and Keith Martin who had kindly agreed to look after the family should Tom and I not make it!), and suggested they get on the next commercial flight to Shannon. Then we took in some local sightseeing.

Angela Recalls:

Mum was very concerned for the whole of the six days Dad took to fly from MinuteMan to Shannon across the North Atlantic. We had never seen her like this! Our normally calm, unflappable Mother was very unsettled and took it out on us kids. In an era before mobile (cell) phones were invented, she did not hear from Dad until the Tuesday when he called from Iceland to say we should get a flight to Ireland the next day. This was a relief to the tension, but he still had the longest and most dangerous leg of the flight to go!

Nevertheless, we boarded the commercial flight (Aer Lingus?) from Boston to Shannon late Wednesday for the overnight flight, not knowing whether he had yet arrived safely. I think Mum was seeing herself as a widow with three young children to bring up!

The Longest Flight

The next morning was bright and clear. We filed a flight plan at 8 a.m. for a scheduled 9 a.m. departure for Shannon, Ireland. With full tanks – thirteen hours' flying – we left Reykjavik on time and set course for Shannon using the VOR outbound radial to check our compass heading for the first two hundred miles.

With a forecast head wind of ten knots, our estimated time en route was seven hours and ten minutes.

The over-ocean leg was about 1,200 miles (nearly 2,000 km) by dead reckoning, so our navigation strategy was to set our heading for the Irish Sea gap between Scotland and Ireland (the mid-point between Glasgow and Belfast) until radio navigation could be established about two hundred miles from the Ireland-Scotland land mass. We then determined our position with a radio fix and re-set course to fly down the west coast of Ireland to the Shannon River and then up the river to Shannon Airport.

Climbing up to our cruising altitude of 8,000 ft., we encountered light turbulence as we passed through a cloud layer and then clear calm conditions on top, just as we headed out over the Atlantic Ocean.

Tom and I settled down with the autopilot maintaining our compass heading, but with the realization that we were traversing a long stretch of water that is notorious for its wildly variable weather and a reputation for some of the worst storms on the planet.

We knew we had done our homework and waited until the weather forecast was in our favour, but this still did not settle our nerves, and we felt somewhat apprehensive.

After about three hours, the weather deteriorated, and the flight was now in solid cloud with moderate turbulence. Is this the start of a storm front that was not anticipated? How bad will it get? Should we consider a course deviation to get around the worst of the weather?

It was the sort of weather that would not be a problem were we over land and near an airport, but in the middle of the Atlantic?

As we pushed through the clouds with zero visibility outside, Tom and I were clearly very anxious until, after an hour, we broke through into clear air with the dark Atlantic below and light blue sky above.

After six hours, we saw the first signs of approaching land when the ADF needle (tuned to a high-power broadcast radio station in Scotland), started to show life and pointed fifteen degrees to the east of our course.

A similar signal from a Northern Ireland radio station enabled us to pinpoint our position on the chart by triangulation and subsequently adjust our heading southwards to fly down the Connemara Coast of Ireland.

Land! – first, some small islands, then the very rugged and rocky coast of Ireland topped by the distinctive green of the Irish pastures.

We flew one hour down the coast, past Galway, then turned left up the Shannon River to land at Shannon Airport at 6.00 p.m. local time, eight hours after departing Reykjavik.

Tom remembers:

When we landed at Shannon, the place was deserted. Apparently, all flights at the time passed through in the morning. When we asked the tower about customs, they just said, 'Welcome to Ireland.'. Then they had us park behind a little office building.

After clearing customs and immigration, Tom and I immediately re-configured the plane by removing the large tank, connecting the smaller tank, and installing the other three seats, making it a five-seat configuration. We then got on two of the bikes and checked into a local B & B at Shannonside and hit the bed exhausted and very satisfied after the long flight across the North Atlantic.

Touring Europe

Our plans for touring Europe on this trip did not include visits to the major cities (been there – done that!), but we did want to visit some of the smaller regional towns and villages with airports close by.

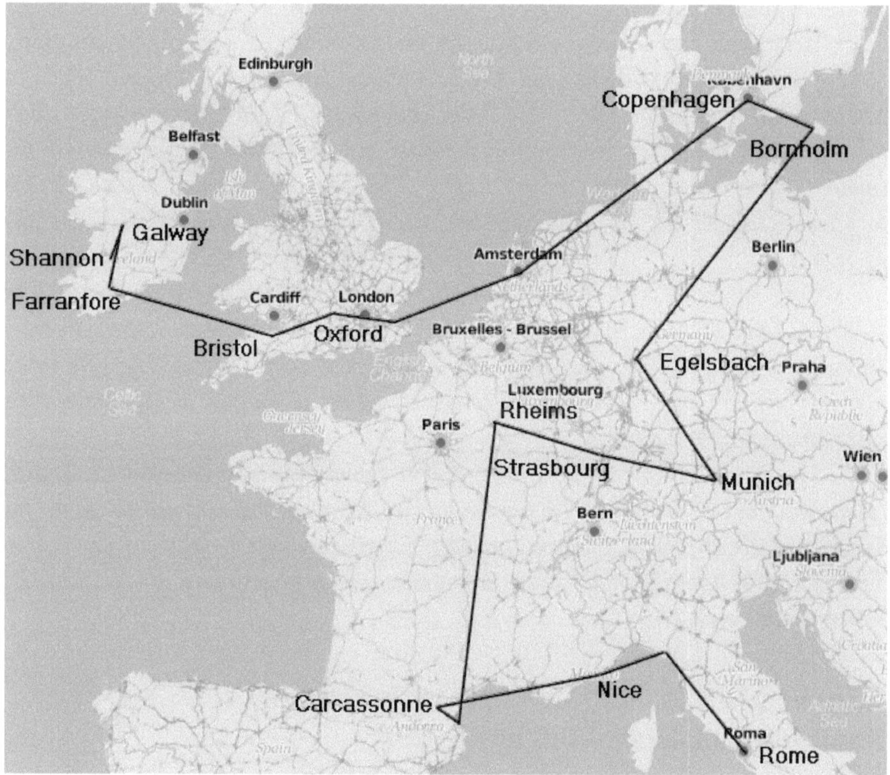

Figure 8 Northern Europe – Ireland to Italy.

The Cessna was to be our inter-city/town transport, and the four fold-up bikes on board were to be our means of travel between the airport and our accommodation in the town and the principal form of travel to the local tourist sites.

Virginia, Angela, and Stuart each had their own bikes, while Rowena sat behind me in a plastic co-pilot child's seat, as she was too young for her own wheels.

Ireland

August 6
Shannon

Virginia's diary:

Robin and Tom arrived at 6 p.m. on August 6, and, after repacking the plane, putting five seats in position, and taking out the large tank, spent the night at Shannonside B & B – adults = £2.00; children = £1.00 (Mrs Tobin) – three miles from the airport on Galway Road. Robin met the commercial airliner with the children and I on board at 9 a.m. on August 7, said farewell to Tom, and we all rode to Shannonside for our first night together. Stuart was sick, and so the following day we rested.

On August 9, we explored Bunratty Castle and Folk Park on the road to Limerick (rode bikes). Castle is small and beautifully restored; several rooms are used for medieval banquets. We were impressed by the spiral stone staircase, dungeons, and old, old furniture and armour inside the castle and by the exterior of the quaint little stone cottages in the park.

However, the interiors were furnished in garish taste (lots of velvet, wallpaper, china dogs, and Victoriana). Then rode back to Shannon and boarded the plane for Galway at about 3 p.m. Galway's airport, Cranmoor, was a half-hour flight from Shannon – a beautiful flight with clear skies and good visibility of the attractive scenery down below.

August 9
Shannon – Galway – 0.5 hrs. – VFR

I knew the airport at Galway (Cranmoor) has a very short E–W runway of 1,500 ft., which is about the minimum length for landing a fully loaded C206, and requires a short field take-off technique with twenty degrees of flaps and full power.

What I did not know until I was in final approach is that there is a high stone wall across the approach near the runway threshold, which required me to 'balloon' the aircraft over the fence, dump it down onto the runway, and then apply the brakes strongly.

Galway

Airport was four miles from the city, and so we rode our bikes and found a good B & B – (Mrs Theresa Quinn). Adults = £2.00; children = £1.50 – one mile from the city. Rode in to the city for dinner at Lydon House Restaurant. Attractive decor here: bits and pieces of armour, windows, swords, etc., adorned the walls. Food was good and about £4.00 for the five of us. The next day, August 10, we explored Galway by bicycle. It was a flourishing seaport (lots of old wharves) until the fifteenth century, but then seemed to become a quiet backwater – not much trade and many people living in poverty. Recently, many companies have started industries here (DEC is one of these) and are bringing work and prosperity to the people.[5] *One or two buildings in Galway are attractive (Lynch's Castle – now a bank – is one), but altogether it's not exceptionally beautiful. The next day, on August 11, we bought four Aran sweaters*[6] *at the Talle shop on Shop Street, visited the bank, and then rode to the airport. Here we realized that we'll have to spend more time in each place as the distance to and from airports and the packing and repacking of the plane is a tiring business. Weather is hot and beautiful. Lunch was wild blackberries that flourished by the airport and popsicles. So on to Killarney.*

August 11
Galway – Farranfore – 0.8 hrs. – VFR
Runway 14/06 – 3,500 ft.

At maximum power and twenty degrees of flaps, we managed to take off from the short Galway airport without wiping off the undercarriage on the stone wall, and then turned south towards Farranfore (Kerry County) airport, the nearest airport to our destination, Killarney.

---

[5] Robin's history note:
With the introduction of Ireland into the European Union in 1973, this period was the start of the technological renaissance for Ireland. The government adopted a strategy of the intensive training of engineers and scientists in the universities and established attractive financial incentives for manufacturers and software houses to set up operations as the base for marketing and distribution into the EU. The success of this strategy was evident when I visited in the early 2000s: Ireland was the runaway growth leader of the EU, with a rapidly growing middle and upper income level population and net positive immigration for the first time since the potato famine in 1849–50.

[6] The Aran sweaters have lasted in the family for thirty-four years and are now being worn by Stuart's sons, Callum and Marcus, and Angela's daughter, Ella.)

As the airport was eight miles (thirteen km) from Killarney, we decided to take our bikes on the local train to ride around Killarney and see the local sites.

Killarney

Arrived at Farranfore airport at 4 p.m. and decided to take a train south with the bikes to Killarney. We spent two days there before flying to England (Bristol, point of entry) via Cork.

The flight to Killarney was beautiful. From the air, we saw large areas of peat bogs, ruins of old churches, lonely farmhouses, and miles of the wonderful green fields. The kids loved the short train trip to Killarney from Farranfore, and, when we arrived, we found, by way of the Irish tourist office, the Drom Hall Hotel – £2.00 per night for adults and children, breakfast included. Today, August 12, we breakfasted early and rode along a tree-lined road to Ross Castle. This is situated in a park on the edge of a lake. The castle is in ruins but is being renovated, and so we could not climb to the top.

We rode along a track through the park to the water's edge, passing by cyclists and people on horses. Angela and I took the wrong turn and got lost. With an undergrowth most lush and beautiful scenery, the mist-covered mountains in the background gave the castle a dreamy air.

We rode back to our hotel for lunch and afterward rode four miles to Muckross Park. We visited the Abbey, a truly wonderful building that suffered at the hands of Cromwell's army during the suppression of monasteries. We saw where the monks ate, cooked, slept, and meditated as well as the main church. All the buildings are made of stone and are still solid, though the church was roofless. It rained during our visit, and now we understand why Ireland is so green: it rains quite frequently here.

From the Abbey, we rode to the main house (no cars allowed here). This house is 150 years old and shows how the Lord of Kerry used to live. We also saw the various industries carried on at his 11,500-acre estate, and it was explained about the Irish way of life at the turn of the century – feudal.

Furniture and finishes in the house were of exquisite quality, and parts of the house were being renovated. We were especially interested in the downstairs Folk Museum where we found a carpenter's shop, stone cutter's shop, dairy, and cobbler's shoemaking shop along with an exhibition of harvesting, other machinery, and the huge kitchen of the house. The gardens were splendid – not a blade of grass out of place and lovely pastel flowers (mainly hydrangeas) growing against the sandstone-faced walls.

Angela recalls:

We all loved seeing the various craft and trade activities, and it reminded us of our visit to Old Sturbridge Village in Western Massachusetts when we were younger.

We had afternoon tea at this house and saw from where we were sitting an Irish currach displayed. The frame of this boat is of wood and then tar-dipped canvas or skin is stretched over. The result is an extremely light and watertight boat.

At our hotel in the evening, we downed gin and tonics at the bar and listened to some good Irish songs. We did the same the previous night also.

Today, 13, we again rode to Muckross Estate and notched up 84 miles (140 km) (total for one week) on our bikes today. We took lunch and rode completely around a lake except for a short two-and-a-half-mile nature walk that we did before lunch.

Figure 9 Lunch in the park – Muckross Estate.

The nature walk was through a yew forest where the trees grew out of moss-covered limestone rocks from the coniferous era. Further on, the soil became very acidic, and nothing much else, except rhododendrons, would flourish there – and they are considered a pest as they are wiping out natural vegetation. Lots of holly bushes here. Does holly grow on other trees? We walked through lovely meadows and finally ended up at an old cottage at the place where waters meet (two lakes meet). It was a wonderful day and we greatly enjoyed the different kinds of woods and forest scenes that we rode through. Many flowers, as well as philodendrons such as foxglove and myrtle, grow wild here.

Went back to town (Killarney) to buy a chicken for supper in our rooms and find out information about buses departing to Farranfore tomorrow. Killarney is a little old town with lots of interesting small shops in side alleys. The smell of horses is everywhere. These animals pull traps and are used to show tourists around – especially for the long trip through Muckross Estate.

August 14, left Killarney by bus for Farranfore, successfully packed aircraft, and flew to Shannon to refuel. Then we flew across Ireland to England at Bristol at 4 p.m.

United Kingdom

August 14
Farranfore – Shannon – Bristol – Oxford
2.9 hrs – VFR then IFR
Refuel stop at Shannon[7]
Customs and Immigration stop at Bristol
Weather: rain clearing at Bristol – some turbulence

Our next stop was to be the university town of Oxford and the Cotswolds tourist area with its well-preserved Roman ruins and architecture.

The nearest airport, Kidlington, is 7 miles (12 km) from Oxford and 2 miles (3.5 km) from Woodstock, the entry town to the Cotswolds.

On departure from Farranfore, we headed east across Ireland in clear conditions, with the emerald green fields of southern Ireland spread out below, before hitting clear air and moderate turbulence over the Irish Sea and along the south coast of Wales and up the Bristol Channel. We landed at Bristol to clear customs and immigration, then it was on to

---

7 These were pre-European Union (EU) days when each country had airports of entry and departure, complete with customs and immigration bureaucracy.

Kidlington (Oxford Airport) where we landed to the north on runway 10. We unpacked the aircraft and cycled into Woodstock.

Oxford

Virginia's diary:

Oxford Airport is situated in the small village of Kidlington, seven miles from Oxford and two miles from the delightful little Cotswold town of Woodstock. We rode on bikes to Woodstock and arrived famished around 6 p.m. The guy at the airport had advised that the King's Head was good for a meal, so we took him at his word. We rode along a narrow street lined with tiny stone cottages until we came to a whitewashed building. This was it, and we were served a wooden platter full of salad, bread, and cheese (stilton and cheddar), fish for Robin, and wine. It was a luscious meal, and the portions were ample in the Olde English style.

After our meal, we found a place to sleep in a charming inn called the Crown Inn. This was used by Oliver Cromwell as a stopping place for re-saddling horses, but since then has been enlarged. It is all built of sandstone and has numerous levels and odd-shaped rooms – but only one bathroom. We had two rooms for £10.00 and slept very well. Breakfast was great – fried bread, tomatoes, sausage, egg and bacon, extra toast, juice, and a huge pot of tea. Angela is now a tea lover.

There are two bars in the pub which come alive after 6 p.m. (in fact, the whole town does), and on our first night we sat in one bar all decorated with airplane stuff, marvellous wooden propellers, etc., and learned that the pub manager had flown three missions for Churchill during the War and afterwards had joined Pathfinders.

August 15' we repacked the airplane in the morning and sent home to Australia two sleeping bags. In the afternoon, we rode to Blenheim Palace just on the outskirts of Woodstock. Blenheim is the home of the Churchill family (Randolph lives there now). The palace is grand to the extreme and was built and presented to the first Lord of Marlborough by Queen Anne, in 1712. We rode through the park (frequently inhabited by sheep and some cattle) and admired the grounds. The children enjoyed a ride on a miniature (real steam) train named Winston Churchill (he was born here). We did not go into the actual palace because of the high price – adults = 70P; children = 50P – but enjoyed the lavish exterior.

For supper that evening, we had fish and chips wrapped in newspaper – everyone loved that – and then a drink in the pub before bed.

The Cotswolds

August 16, we rode to Kidlington and rented an Austin Allegro for the weekend for £12.00 in order to tour the Cotswolds. We drove for miles through tiny and large villages and beautiful countryside. The villages were completely built of stone and most charming, flowers and creepers covering walls and most of the buildings very old. The roofs of the buildings were covered either in slate or cut stone shingles.

We drove from Woodstock to Chipping Norton, Stowe on the Wold, Cheltenham, and then Cirencester. At Cirencester, we booked in at Raydon Guest House – £8.00 per night B & B – and then walked a short distance to view the archaeological digs of Corinium Dobunnorum, which was a large Roman camp and city (280 acres) underneath part of Cirencester (cester = camp in Roman) that was only smaller than the Roman city of Lendmin (340 acres). It was fascinating to see a partly exposed shopping mall and many other buildings, and we resolved the next day to visit the Roman Villa at Chedworth.

Cirencester is a large town – the major one in the Cotswolds and most attractive with the usual lovely sandstone buildings – well-kept with brightly painted windows and door trims.

August 17, we rose early and after a substantial breakfast of eggs, bacon, and tomato set off for the villa.

The villa is only partly exposed and is large and must have been a luxurious county house. It was equipped with many sauna-type bathing facilities, both hot wet steam and dry steam and cold immersion baths to cool off and close the pores afterwards. The heating facilities for the dining and entertainment rooms were most advanced: we saw how the furnace heated underground air that was then forced through flow vents at the base of interior walls. Hollow ceramic bricks were used for the vents, and some floors were raised on ceramic or stone piles to allow the hot air to circulate freely underneath.

Stuart recalls:

I was amazed that they had under-floor heating via ducts during the Roman occupation of Britain.

There was also a kitchen (with baking oven) and a bathroom with latrines. Sponges tied to long sticks were used instead of toilet paper, and they were flushed in running water. All of these described rooms, plus more that may have been bedrooms, were placed around two courts (an inner and an outer court). Not to be forgotten were the intricate patterns created in tiny ceramic and stone tiles on the floors of the dining room, entertainment area, and one of the bathrooms. The tiles were mostly cut from local rock, in colours of white, blue, purple, and black and terracotta tiles were used for red.

We also visited the museum that was filled with a fascinating array of odds and ends from the site: old coins, carpenters' tools (much like our present-day ones), broken pieces of ceramic pots, animal bones (from a trash heap so that we could tell what the Romans ate for dinner), and many other things.

We then drove to Staverton airport to have a delicious lunch of pastries and to view an exhibition called Skyfame of famous and unusual old aircraft. We all loved this as it was possible to climb up and view the inside of most of these old machines and then afterwards, in a little back room, to see hundreds of models of little airplanes. The kids loved this, especially Stuart, and it was the highlight of his day. He wants to make up similar models and have them arranged all around his room. He would have stayed all day. Also exhibited were many World War II air force posters and photographs that were interesting to us all and yet seemed so far away from the life we lead today.

Then it was back into the car again and off to visit Sudeley Castle, whose history dates back to Saxon times. We saw an interesting light-and-sound display here of the Tudor monarchs who were involved with Sudeley (Catherine Parr is buried in its exquisite chapel with lovely stained glass windows). The castle was partly destroyed in Cromwellian times and now has partly been restored (lovely museum), and the rest had been made into gardens.

It is easy to imagine a Tudor count living there, and we saw notices that there is to be a joust on August 24. We were charged inflated prices to go into this castle, but it was well worth every penny as the gardens were superb (formal garden with old-fashioned plants especially). After leaving Sudeley, we winded our way back into the beautiful Cotswold Hills in order to spend the night in Stow on the Wold. Unfortunately, we couldn't afford the high prices of that town (my favourite) and so ended up at one of its neighbours, Moreton in the Wood. The Cotswolds are more beautiful than I had believed, and I think even Robin was impressed for he said that the scenery here has a permanence that one doesn't see in USA (Mass., I expect) – perhaps that is because of the stone buildings here. Fabulous weekend in the Cotswolds that I will never forget.

Stayed the night in a B & B at Moreton in the Wood for £2.25 each.

Oxford – Southend – 1.0 hr. – VFR

Just as the UK had an airport of entry at the time, it also has designated airports of departure for flights to Europe. Ours was Southend.

As our next leg was to Copenhagen, 4.5 hrs., we chose to split the journey and fly from Oxford to Southend on the eighteenth and park the aircraft while we visited London for four days, then clear customs and immigration on departure for Copenhagen.

We departed Oxford on an easterly heading across the north of London to Southend-on-Sea, which is on the lower North Sea coast.

I filed an IFR flight plan to ensure I had radar guidance from Heathrow traffic controllers. I didn't want to get tied up with the heavy commercial aircraft on final approach to Heathrow!

> *August 18, left Moreton in the Wood early by car for Kidlington to return the car and then packed the bikes in the plane. Rob flew the plane to Southend airport, one hour by train from London (port of departure for Copenhagen). A long day's travel as we had a two-mile walk to the station at Southend, a trip by train to Liverpool Station and by central underground to Douglas Mansions (Station Gloucester Road), a hostel. Cheap, cheap – adults = £2.75; children = £1.72 – and very central, right in Kangaroo Valley. It's very seedy and derelict, but at least is a bed.*

London

> *August 19, breakfasted on rolls and coffee in the basement and then caught the tube into Victoria Station. Here we boarded a bus and did a two-hour London Transport Tour of this huge and sprawling city. Among other things, we saw Thames Embankment, Cleopatra's Needle, No. 10 Downing Street, Houses of Parliament, the Tate Gallery, and other landmarks of note. Went past everything too quickly to gain more than a quick impression, but it did give us an idea of the immensity of the city.*
>
> *After a meat pie for lunch, we walked to Buckingham Palace's gates and looked in – it wasn't possible to see over. We then walked through Knightsbridge and caught a bus to Kensington Gardens, saw the Antique Supermarket (Robin was impressed) but could not get into London Museum as it was undergoing renovations. Instead, we saw over some of Queen Victoria's apartments at Kensington Palace (magnificent panelling designed by Sir Christopher Wren) and many other works of art. The kids then saw*

an outdoor puppet show and played in a park before we walked home through embassy diplomats' homes and through Kensington to a delicious take-out Chinese meal.

August 20, up early and off by tube to see the Tower of London. We spent the whole morning here, seeing parts of the tower and viewing old walls of the Roman period that are being excavated, the Crown Jewels and precious gold plate, and an extensive exhibition of armour and guns. Tomorrow we go back to see more of the Tower. After lunch, we went to the Theatre Royal at Drury Lane to see the musical Billy. This was a great treat for all of us. We were in the upper circle (seats £1.90 each) and could enjoy the opulence of the theatre décor before the show began.

Billy (Michael Crawford) is a most imaginative young man (a liar also) who has wonderful dreams of becoming a scriptwriter in London. He and his best girlfriend, Liz, plan to go to London, but, when the moment finally comes to board the train, he is unable to go. Instead, he retreats into his dream world of Ambrosia where he is president. Everything was great about this show, and it always centred on Billy, who had, by far, the major part. The composer (John Barry) of the music also wrote 'Born Free' and 'Goldfinger'.

After this exciting day, we returned home (home is where we live at present) for a picnic supper with plans to get visas and visit Australia House for mail tomorrow.

August 21, this day we planned a full itinerary, starting with the Tower again. Instead, we finished up having a very varied day and didn't see any of the tourist sights.

First stop was the Indonesian embassy in Park Lane to try for a tourist visa and to understand more about the mysteries of flying a private aircraft in Indonesia. The embassy required three days to process the visa and also evidence of intent to enter and leave country (ticket), so our visit was unsuccessful. We need to obtain prior permission for aircraft first, so will proceed down this path.

Next, visited Burmese embassy, with same result. These two countries need a lot more work before we can finalize the red tape.

Figure 10 Virginia and kids outside Australia House.
It was lunchtime, and the kids were obviously hungry.

Had lunch of pies in a small park and then headed towards Australia House. On the way, passed a camera shop with two second-hand cameras on display. On impulse, bought single-lens reflex camera for £36 (F2-8, 1/1000 sec), looks like a reasonable bargain. At Australia House, picked up our mail redirected by Audrey, including pay cheque, then caught a London taxi to London Design Centre. Purchased presents for nephews and nieces. Returned to hostel for dinner of bread, salami, cheese, and honey-dew melon.

Angela remembers:

For the trip, Mum purchased bright-coloured, easy to wash and dry, T-shirts with zip necks: Angela, blue; Stuart, red; and Rowena, yellow. She said that the bright colours were so that we would not get lost in the crowds. We wore these virtually every day, and Mum washed them at night for use again the next day.

August 22, up early and straight to the Tower to complete the visit started on Wednesday. Spent most of time at the armouries looking at armour and arms.

After lunch of pies and coffee, boarded a boat for Westminster, passing by a number of tourist sights seen from the road on Tuesday. At Westminster, confined our visit to the Abbey, which drained the last of our physical reserves after a tough week (too bad, as there was an international exhibit of model railroads across the way from the Abbey). Home to a supper of Kentucky Fried Chicken and chips followed by lemon tarts and ice cream.

Southend – Copenhagen – 4.6 hrs.
August 23

We departed Southend for the eighty-five–mile trip across the English Channel to Amsterdam. There was good weather as far as Amsterdam and then we ran into rain, clouds, and build-ups. We had icing at 9,000 ft., so we dropped to 7,000 ft. which solved the problem. We flew across the farmlands of the north of Germany and then into Danish-controlled air space. The weather was good into Copenhagen where we landed just in front of a DC-9 on final approach. The Copenhagen controllers are very efficient and expect good knowledge on the part of the pilots.

Virginia's diary:

The scenery is most interesting when flying over Holland. The land is like a pudding basin, becoming lower at the centre. Rich farmlands are divided by canals – very neat tidy countryside. Saw the Zuiderzee Dyke – most impressive.

Denmark

Airport of Entry: Copenhagen / Kastrup
100 KR ($16) landing fee; 6 KR ($1) per night
Very busy airport – heavies – took off between two DC-8s

We had pre-arranged to stay at a B & B owned by Fay and Gyde Sorensen at Virum, a northern outer suburb of Copenhagen. We caught a train from the airport to Virum and then walked to the B & B.

Copenhagen

August 24, Stuart's birthday. Had a leisurely breakfast and walk around the lake at Virum. Mrs Sorensen is American (first generation, from Denmark before that). Mr Sorensen is Danish and so is son Kurt, fifteen.

Caught the train from Virum at noon after an extensive walk. We passed by some marvellous and expensive apartments that I think I read about in the Age (Melbourne's daily newspaper) years ago. Had lunch in the city and said goodbye to Robin who went to the airport to get papers from the plane. The kids and I strolled down the Stroget – the kids very interested in and I tried to ignore the pornographic shops and cinemas, fascinating. Met Robin outside Tivoli at 3 p.m. and spent four hours strolling in this old-fashioned, elegant, and fun park; listening to two band shows and small orchestras; and watching two acts by tumblers and acrobats. All entertainment was of top-class calibre and most enjoyable.

The Tivoli was quite crowded, mostly older people and people with kids. We wondered where the young swingers were. The gardens were spectacular – many unusual flowers and combinations of them. That is what I enjoyed most.

Angie and Stuart remember:

We visited Tivoli gardens, the oldest theme park in the world (from 1843), set amongst beautiful gardens and buildings. We went on all the rides, including a Ferris wheel and roller coaster. There were acrobats, clowns, and jugglers on the streets. The treat at the end was a really huge ice cream in a Danish waffle cone. We all felt it was a bit like fairy-land with all the beautiful lights in the trees and stunning gardens with amazing combinations of flowers. We stayed until night when there was a fireworks display. We stayed with friends in an A-frame house. The friends had amazing government benefits and free holidays.

Virginia's diary:

August 25, Monday and shops open, so Stuart can at least get his penknife for his birthday gift. We went by S train to Copenhagen in the late morning, bought food for lunch at the station at Virum, and ate it by the town hall – most pleasant. Robin does the shopping and buys the most luscious things; he says it's cheaper than dining in restaurants and, we all think, far nicer. After lunch, we looked in at a Volvo showroom. View getting one shipped to Australia, but no go – import taxes are too high.

Next we walked down the Stroget and looked in shops for watches and silver chains for me. We finally got to Magasin du Nord (Stuart nearly crazy with impatience by this time) to check out the penknives. Purchased Swiss Army knife for him and a lovely cube and link chain for me – the latter much too expensive, but I love it. Also bought delicacies for supper and set off to walk around the old part of town and find a suitable place to eat.

Stuart recalls:

For the rest of the trip my new penknife was very handy to cut up the salami which we usually bought for our picnic lunches.

This we did at the palace on the edge of the fountain, and it was quite beautiful, water everywhere and kids running around the edge. Had another walk after supper and then back home to bed.

August 26, today was quite perfect – still having good weather. We decided to go to Roskilde. This means a twenty-mile trip into the city and change of trains and then a twenty-mile trip on a fast train north-west to the Royal Country seat. It's at the end of a fjord and is in an old and pretty town.

The train we came on is fast and clean, with lovely tweed-like upholstered seats and small trays and drink rests that slide out from the arms.

First we got some lunch food at a large and interesting supermarket and then Robin arranged a $60 bank draft to pay the Indonesians for letting us fly over their country. After we had picnicked, we walked down through the town on old roads and by a bicycle path to the Viking Museum that is an attractive contemporary structure situated right at the water's edge. Here are housed 5,900-year-old ships that have been raised to the surface. They were originally sunk in an area (to block the fjord and so stop any enemies from invading the Queen's castle) to cause a dam almost across the fjord from depths of 1.5 to 5 ft. and have been cleaned down, treated with glycol to stop shrinkage, all the parts placed together (like a jigsaw puzzle) and assembled as much as possible, and placed on view.

Also available for us to see were the workshops where all this took place, an extensive gallery of photographs; information, and old maps to show how far the Vikings had travelled and whom they had conquered; and a film about the actual finding, raising, cleaning, and restoration of the boats. The finding and the raising up the boats took place during their brief summer period.

We then walked along by the shore, looking at the yachts and fishing boats and discussing their merits. After that, a play in the children's park for the kids, another tasty and interesting supper (we tried some Danish pastries), and then two train trips home.

Mrs Sorensen's son Kurt has since told us that in recent years (I guess since skin-diving equipment has become available) many Viking ships have been discovered along the coastlines of Denmark, and the government could not possibly afford to raise them all up: the soft mud under the water in which they lie is a good preservative, so there they will stay.

August 27, spent a wonderful day at the Folk Museum at Lyngby. This was a short bus ride from Virum. Here, set in pleasant farmlands, is a collection of Danish farmhouses from all over Denmark that have been brought, dismantled (each piece numbered) and then carefully rebuilt at this site. Houses 300–500 years old. There were about forty farm buildings here, including a fisherman's cottage and a gristmill.

Figure 11 Thatched cottages at Lyngby Folk Museum.

We decided against taking the English-language tour and instead, after a delicious picnic, looked at each house ourselves. We particularly noticed that many of the older houses had mud floors and walls made primarily of mud and stones (painted over) between the old wood supports. As time wore on (or if the farm houses had been prosperous) there was use of cobbled or wood block or brick or wood plank flooring, and the walls were more wooden than mud and, sometimes, even of brick.

As the houses were so old, they mostly leaned at odd angles and were all utterly charming. They must have been of sound construction as some had been standing on the present site since 1920.

The roofs were mainly thatched or of peat sod. At one cottage we found some pigs that the kids named 'Salami', 'Bacon', and 'Roast Pork'. In some cottages, weaving and candle making were in process. We particularly noticed the large number of artefacts present, all kinds of tools and quite small things found in homes. Obviously a lot of care had gone into setting this up. Each artefact, however, was glued or nailed to a surface, and when Robin tried to remove something for inspection an alarm sounded and a guard appeared.

The houses were mainly painted white, some a deep red ochre colour with black trim and some a golden yellow ochre, traditional Danish colours.

After our day in the picturesque folk museum, we bought more food and ate on a hillside by a church on the way to Virum. Robin has spoiled us by getting different kinds of Danish pastries for us to try at each meal. My waistline is suffering, but my appetite is not.

It's our last night with the hospitable Sorensens. We've learned that as well as their son Kurt who has just started at a two-year college they have a son Kenneth (seventeen) who is retarded and has muscular dystrophy and who is in hospital with tracheotomy after pneumonia. Mrs Sorensen is ever so cheerful and has taken in people ever since her boys were young. She was home so much with Kenneth, she said it was one way to meet and be with people. She is mentioned in Europe on $10.00 per day and also takes in US students who come to study at Danish universities for one semester. Gyde is a retired army major who is in real estate at Virum.

Copenhagen – Bornholm (Ronne) – 0.7 hrs. – VFR

The small Danish island of Bornholm, forty minutes from Copenhagen in the Baltic Sea, south of Sweden, was our next destination for three days of rest and relaxation.

We landed at the airport at Ronne, the capital of this small municipality, and then cycled the 2 miles (3.5 km) into the town centre to seek accommodation.

August 28, we left early in Faye's Prinz for the station, said our goodbyes, and rode back to Copenhagen where we boarded the S.A.S. bus to the airport. There was not much delay while Robin filed a flight plan and then we headed out from Copenhagen over the tip of Sweden and over the balmy blue for half an hour until we came to the Danish island of Bornholm. We then rode bikes to the town of Ronne and found a comfortable house to sleep. The owners speak no English, but not to worry.

August 29, a beautiful nothing day spent on the beach at Ronne. All we are doing is acquiring a suntan, playing, and catching up with correspondence.

August 30, enjoying staying with the Danish couple, who are most friendly. Each morning, Robin goes off to the shop across the road and comes back with delicious Danish pastries and apple juice for breakfast.

Figure 12 The round church of Bornholme.

After breakfast in our rooms and coffee at the cafeteria in town, we set off to ride to Arnager, a nearby seaside village near the airport, to see some ancient burial places; no sign of these, but we enjoyed the sparkling water, attractive houses, and lunch on a hilltop before riding off to see one of the historic round churches in Bornholm.

They were built from AD 1100 as fortifications and food storage areas as well as for worship, and we were able to climb up narrow stairs to see the two huge circular rooms above the main area of worship on the ground floor. This was very simple and beautiful, whitewashed with simple pews, all with vases of fresh flowers at the end of them. The central pillar was decorated with a fresco, and there were two or three small pictures of angels on the walls (very old). The church grounds were well kept, and lovely simple gravestones with well-tended gardens were in evidence.

Lovely sunny weather all the time in Bornholm, and we all found ourselves enjoying local ice creams and becoming a little suntanned.

Angela remembers:

We were reminded of previous trips to Nantucket Island as kids. We rode around on our bikes, and it felt safe. And we played on the beach. There was an 'old' lady who stripped naked (as the Danes do) and went for a swim in the cold surf. She had an all-over tan.

Virginia's diary:

August 31, plane washday. We rode to the airport, changed into swimsuits, and then proceeded to wash the plane with Jergens soap, water, brushes, and rags, plus gas for the oily streaks. At twelve noon or so, we picnicked, then finished the plane and took off for a short tour of Bornholm, circumnavigating the island and now able to see the ruins of a castle at the north of the island and the other three towns on the west of the island. The entire interior is either forests or lovely old farms with farm buildings built in the traditional style.

After our flight, we spent two hours at a beach near the airport, swimming and soaking up the sun. Rob and I were amused at the cultural differences in Scandinavia where it is quite okay to change for a swim right on the beach. The kids built a big dam and seemed to have a great time. Then back to our favourite Qvickly cafeteria for fish and chips for supper and then home to bed.

Germany

Bornholm – Egelsbach (Germany) – 4.2 hrs – VFR on top Egelsbach is a small village 10 miles (16 km) south of Frankfurt

Departed Bornholm at 10 a.m. in hazy conditions with a climb out to 9,000 ft. Our flight plan took us west initially to avoid flying over what was then the German Democratic Republic (GDR) and being shot down by Soviet fighter planes, then we turned south on course to Frankfurt. Weather conditions were overcast, and we were flying on top of the cloud cover.

With the IFR flight plan and no instrument approach to Egelsbach, air traffic control directed us to make an ILS approach to Frankfurt Airport to get under the cloud layer. Then they provided us with radar vectors towards Egelsbach and a smooth VFR landing.

We had chosen Egelsbach because it is a light aircraft airport with good flight facilities and point-of-entry customs and immigration capabilities.

The village of Egelsbach is only a short bike ride away and has a train service to the hub at Frankfurt, so this is where we chose to stay the first night in the Rhine region.

Virginia's diary:

September 1, off to the airport again as we are bound for Egelsbach, Germany, this time and from there to the Rhine River for four days touring. Weather is good and not a long wait at the airport before take-off. Am crabby and miserable with a fever, and the kids fought all the way on our four-hour trip to Germany. We were all glad to land at 2.30 p.m. – hungry.

Rode through Egelsbach and, with the help of a young boy, found an inexpensive Italian-run hotel in which to spend the night. Me, exhausted with flu. Robin, tired too but somehow managed to muster energy to put together a lovely meal for us from the supermarket in many varieties of sausage and German bread. Kids, very helpful and fascinated by how things are different in a new country.

September 2, up bright and early, a good beginning to a rather frustrating day. We found out that the first train that would take our bikes left for Frankfurt at 12.20 p.m. We played in a park all morning and were ready for the train, but a guard would not let us on.

Figure 13 A Pause for play.

The next train was one hour later. Changed at Frankfurt and had a fast trip of one hour to Rudesheim. Very healthy vineyards along the way; rail and road following the river. Reached Rudesheim and booked in at hotel. Rudesheim is very touristy – souvenir shops and cafes everywhere – prices high and people thronging in the narrow picturesque streets. Roofs in town all of real slate and local stone.

Rob went out and bought food, and, after a substantial picnic, we went to sleep. Rob fixed his new camera that had got sand in it at Bornholm.

September 3, up bright and early and breakfasted in hotel. Today we rode eleven miles to Kaub, a lovely small town not spoilt by the tourist trade. Ate lunch there and then searched for somewhere to sleep. Found it in old house built into the cliff – $20 equivalent for bed and breakfast, but no bath. Our nice rooms were on the ground floor, and our lavish breakfast the next day of rolls, bread, salami, cheese, jam, boiled eggs, and coffee was served on the fourth floor.

Before describing our day, a little about the Rhine must be written. This is an exciting river, always alive with passing traffic, coal barges, luxury steamers carrying people touring from Holland, and many others. Ferries cross from one side to the other regularly, especially if there is a town on either side. Along the banks on each side run railroad tracks, kept busy by long freight trains that lug everything from cars to animals and people on the fast passenger train from Frankfurt to Koblenz. Along each bank, at not too far apart intervals, are small picturesque towns, all old and the buildings have slate roofs. Many castles, either partly or wholly in ruins, cling to hillsides and ledges. These are all full of history of the days when to ride the Rhine was to have great power in Europe.

After lunch, on September 3, we left our bikes at the hotel and climbed high on a winding road to Burg Gutenfels, a small castle that is set among steep vineyards. The castle, partly in ruins, is not open to the public, but banquets are held there.

Figure 14 Rhine River from Burg Gutenfels Castle

We walked around the castle and saw the drawbridge and other battlements. I wish I could have gone inside (someone was living there).

We trekked around the mountainside, sampling the rather bitter grapes and deciding that to make wine is a lot of hard work, in the early stages anyway. The ground is so steep that to plough the furrows a tractor is parked at the top that lets down a steel cable that is attached to a plough. The man stands behind the plough, walks and guides it, but the winch attached to the tractor pulls the plough up. I really loved that walk; it was hot, heavy, and humid, and the mist that had lain around the river all day had lifted so that now the sky was bright blue and contrasted with the bright light green of the vineyards.

Robin bought a bottle of Rhine wine for us to try that night that was really good even though unchilled.

Figure 15 Two hundred miles on our bikes and an ice cream celebration.

September 4, left Kaub after the hearty breakfast described before and rode on to St Goar. At Lonely Rock, Stuart became tired, so we stopped. Discovered that we'd passed the two hundred-mile mark on our bikes and so had to celebrate. Ice creams all round at 10.30 a.m. – quite a treat.

At St Goar, we decided not to proceed to Koblenz as first intended but to ride across the river by ferry, check into a hotel, explore the large castle on the hillside, and, the following day, pedal our way back towards Mainz. This we did. Our hotel this time doesn't have a bath (same as previous one) and *also doesn't have any hot water in taps, but, apart from that, is a superb value for $20 for five for one night and breakfast.*

After a lunch of bratwurst and bread, we commenced the 1-km steep ascent of Burg Rheinfels, the largest castle on the Rhine and quite a fascinating one. We did two walking tours of this large group of buildings; one outside examining battlements, etc., and one inside seeing rooms and a museum. The fortifications of these buildings are fantastic. In fact, we walked back into town by following one of the walls, and at every few feet in the wall were openings both vertical and horizontal for archers. The castle was built in the thirteenth century, and part of it was 'done up' and added on to in the sixteenth century; since then it seemed to have fallen into decay until 1956 when interest in this huge castle was revived once more. The corridors, large and small rooms, stone house, etc., are fantastic in size and number: it must have sheltered many thousands of people when in use.

Tonight we had our customary picnic. Poor Robin's wrist must get tired as he has so many slices of food to cut. The kids are always very hungry. After all enjoyed another pastry, I washed clothes (heated water in a jug with element) and then hung them on the roof to dry.

September 5, the day was overcast and raining, so we decided to forget our plans to bicycle back down the Rhine (at least part of the way) and instead go straight by train to Frankfurt. No hitches here. Robin is good at deciphering railroad timetables now and showed me which trains had provision for bikes. We enjoyed the trip back again, though glad we rode up the right side as the road on the left side was not always close to the river. It was fascinating and different scenery, and, as usual, there was a contrast of the busy river to the peaceful and well-ordered look of the vineyards on the hillsides.

Figure 16 Rhine River vineyards.

We got to Frankfurt at lunchtime and ate lunch half at Frankfurt and half at Egelsbach before riding the two kilometres to airport. Had a short wait here while Robin paid Cessna for the oil change and engine check and filled out papers, but soon we were off to Munich at 3.30 p.m.

Egelsbach – Munich – 1.6 hrs. – VFR on top

Munich was a deviation from our policy of small towns for our European tour as Virginia and the kids had heard about the Deutsches Museum[8], the largest technology museum in the world, from friends and expressed a desire to visit.

---

8 The Deutsches Museum (German Museum) in Munich, Germany, is the world's largest museum of technology and science, with approximately 1.5 million visitors per year and about 28,000 exhibited objects from 50 fields of science and technology. The museum was founded on June 28, 1903, at a meeting of the Association of German Engineers (VDI) as an initiative of Oskar von Miller. The full name of the museum in

We filed an IFR flight plan at Egelsbach and climbed out through the overcast to cruise to Munich at 9,000 ft. on top of the cloud.

Our approach to Munich airport was through the cloud for a full ILS approach and landing.[vi]

The bikes stayed in the aircraft while we caught a taxi to Munich Railway Station as a base for locating accommodation.

Virginia's diary:

> *Arrived at Munich airport, and by 6.00 p.m. Robin had found, at the Munich train station, a selection of hotels to choose from. We located in the Marie-Luise Hotel Pension close to station. Sixty DM per night for five in one room and continental breakfast seemed reasonable by high-priced Munich standards. All had red bokwirst mit brod for supper and sank gratefully into bed that night.*

Munich

> *September 6, unanimous decision today to visit the world-renowned Deutsches Museum. This is a technological museum and is huge and fantastic. It shows everything man has ever done and is doing now – both old-fashioned method or design and current one. It is impossible to see in one day, and that is why I'm sure the entrance fee is so low – 2 DM for adults, 50 F for children – so that one would be tempted to visit again and again. We spent the whole day here from 10 a.m. till the doors closed at 5 p.m. and then slunk home exhausted and dropped into bed.*
>
> *September 7, the family wanted to go again to the museum, and I can see why, so we did. I sat and wrote postcards during the morning to rest the old legs but walked around in the pm. The most exciting things about this museum are: the numerous press button exhibitions that really work particularly in the chemistry department; the complete exhibition of real underground mines, coal, salt, and potash; the wonderful dioramas and models in such exhibitions as hydraulics and heavy engineering; the walk-in*

English is German Museum of Masterpieces of Science and Technology (German: *Deutsches Museum von Meisterwerken der Naturwissenschaft und Technik*). It is the largest museum in Munich.
Source: Wikipedia

airplane, ship, and submarine exhibits; and the large and extensive group of automobiles and trains, and much, much more.

Angela remembers:

Deutsches Technological Museum – two days of it! It is the largest technology and science museum in the world and had exhibitions such as a fully functioning mine, an Apollo 8 space capsule, and the history of just about everything. As children, we loved all the push-button experiments with a range of chemical reactions.

Dined at McDonald's Munich tonight (reason, inexpensive). Prices are double those in United States for McDonald's food, but it was most enjoyable though. We walked home through the main streets of Munich to our hotel. It is a most attractive city, mostly of modern design, made bright and colourful by many fountains and large tubs of flowers (mainly begonias and impatiens – brightly coloured).

France

Munich – Strasbourg – Rheims – 4.0 hrs. – VFR on top

Our next destination was to be Rheims, in the Champagne area of France. But to get there, we again had to pass through an airport of entry – this time Strasbourg on the French side of the Rhine River.

We departed Munich on an IFR flight plan and again climbed out to cruise on top of the overcast.

Approaching the Germany-France border, we called up the French flight controller to report position, but they had no trace of our flight plan!

I re-filed a flight plan in the air and then received clearance to approach and land at Strasbourg.

The fact that the French controllers had misplaced my flight plan did not surprise me as I had heard that they are fiercely independent. When I made initial contact, they responded with a 'Bonjour, monsieur', and then proceeded to issue instructions in French despite English being the standard language for international air traffic control. When I responded in English, I found that they could speak English after all!

On departure from Strasbourg, the alternator failed to show any charging of the battery, so I had no alternative but to turn back and get it repaired.

This made us late into Rheims, and we rode into town to find accommodation in the gathering dusk at 8.00 p.m.

Rheims

Virginia's diary:

September 8, departed early for flight to Rheims via Strasburg and caught Lufthansa bus to airport. There was some commotion at the departure of a large jet near our plane. Armed guards were posted on the tarmac, an armed truck was standing by, and a search was made of the plane before it took off. The flight was good to Strasburg and only one-hour long. Arrived at lunchtime and finally got a ham sandwich at 1.30 p.m. after talking to customs, flight-planning people, etc. Left at 2.30 p.m. for Rheims VFR and had been in the air about five minutes when Rob discovered an electrical fault in the plane, so we returned to Strasburg and a friendly Piper engineer repaired the fault – for no charge. So at 5 p.m., after another drink of coffee, we departed for Rheims one-and-a-half hours away.

The electrical fault in the engine was the failure of the alternator to charge the battery. The engineer discovered a wire had fallen off the alternator due to vibration. He reconnected the wire and all was OK.

Arrived at Rheims at 6.30 p.m. to the tune of jet fighters practicing take-offs and landings. Unpacked bikes and rode the five km into Rheims in approaching darkness. Arrived at about 8 p.m. and checked into Champagne à Accual on Avenue de Paisc – two rooms (six beds) and bathroom for $16, no breakfast, and central location. Breakfast was 4 F extra and a rip-off. Everyone was tired and dirty and loved their first baths in a week.

September 9, Robin says Rheims is the size of Hobart; it is an attractive place dominated by the champagne industry and Rheims Cathedral. The latter we visited, and it is very beautiful – starkly simple inside but with lovely carved stone figures and unusual stained glass windows in brilliant colours. The cathedral was excessively damaged in WW I, and the windows are new additions. Also, there are many wonderful old tapestries on the walls depicting different aspects of medieval life. Had a quick bicycle tour around the city and put together our usual good lunch. Everyone was enthusiastic about the French breadsticks.

Stuart got stuck in the male toilet in a large department store. The handle was off his door, so I stood up on a heater to try and set him free. Unfortunately, I released the tap, and we had water pouring out as well as a locked-up boy. A French gentleman and two startled ladies came to our assistance, but Stuart was able to set himself free.

We then rode across town to Mumm's to have a free tour of their champagne cellars and a demonstration of various stages of champagne making, including two fermentations, bottle shaking, freezing the sediment and removing it, replacing extra-sweetened liquor, and capping with a cork and muzzle.

Angela remembers:

Rhiems – went to Mumm's champagne house and was fascinated by the production process. This included freezing the top sediment to remove impurities. We were also interested in the fact that all workers got free champagne off the line. Everyone got a taste of champagne.

Bike riding was bumpy over the cobblestones in French villages, and we felt very giddy from our first taste of champagne.

Virginia's diary:

We walked down deep into the hand-dug chalk cellars and saw thousands of bottles maturing and the old- and new-fashioned ways of corking and then shared a bottle of Red Label Brut (US$8.50) with the other members of the party. A special sweet champagne was opened for the kids and two other members of the party. Apparently, workers at Mumm's who all come from the Champagne area are given a bottle of real wine each day to discourage the drinking of the product that they manufacture, also free champagne on all religious and festive occasions. It was quite a day, and we all felt lightheaded. The champagne was wonderful and so were the cellars. Had a picnic supper and then went out to coffee with Robin and a look at the shops – most attractive but expensive merchandise.

September 10, had breakfast in our rooms with the help of the café from below and then set out for a 30-km ride around part of the champagne area.

Our route was as follows: Rheims → Montferre → Chigny Les Roses (where we ate lunch) → Rilly la Montagne → Montferre → Rheims.

For the most part, we rode past rows and rows of cultivated blue grape vines, very pretty and well cared for, and country with pretty wildflowers growing by the side of the road. We saw lone workers or sometimes groups pruning the vines that will be ready for harvesting at the end of September. The ride was over hilly country, and the main champagne-growing area is roughly horseshoe shaped south of Rheims. When we stopped for lunch, a crowd of little French boys joined us, and we talked about bikes and our trip.

Figure 17 A pause at a village near Rheims.

It was a very pleasant day, and, when we returned to the hotel at 3 p.m., Robin and I were tired – but not the kids. Had another picnic supper and then rode into the city in the dusk for coffee at a sidewalk café.

Carcassonne
Rheims – Carcassonne – 3.7 hrs. – IFR
Weather: cumulus clouds en route

Log notes:

Departed Rheims on IFR flight plan, VFR conditions. Paris control routed us around Paris. Hot day, cumulus clouds particularly over a central range of mountains up to 4,000 ft. high. Headed towards Perpignan, then cancelled IFR and spiralled down from 9,000 ft. to get under overcast. Followed road, rail, and canal to Carcassonne at 2,000 ft. Landed VFR. Good airport.

Virginia's diary:

Carcassonne: September 11, flew from Rheims (after riding to the airport and Angela had a puncture on the way), a three-and-a-half-hour flight to the South of France – Carcassonne, whose old medieval city we planned to visit. The kids were good (quiet) during the flight that was interesting geographically to us because we discovered a range of mountains down the centre of France. We were flying through cloud, and suddenly it cleared and high peaks could be seen below.

Weather was good all the way, and, when we landed at Carcassonne, it was warm, although not with much sun. Straightaway, one notices that Spain is close by. People's skin is darker, houses have red terracotta tile roofs, and life is slower, as Denis, the head of the flight school at Carcassonne, said when he welcomed us.

We rode the five km into the town and located a hotel, Hotel Bernard, right in the centre of town – two rooms plus five beds, no bathroom or breakfast, for $10 per night. Added to this was the benefit of parking spaces where the kids could play and the bikes could be kept.

Tonight we had pâté and bread and fruit, raisin juice and wine, and ice cream and had a quick walk before getting to sleep.

September 12, we woke early, washed, and breakfasted (the kids were anxious to use the extra piece of plumbing in the bathroom) and then rode our bicycles through the town to the hill on which La Cite is built. We pushed our bikes up the hill and parked them before entering by the drawbridge and exploring. La Cite is a completely walled, well-preserved, and lived-in (by 1,000 inhabitants) city that dates back to the fifth, tenth and twelfth centuries. Some of its walls are even older – Roman. It is fascinating to see a wall that three or four different groups of people in different times have built; we saw the same thing at the Tower of London.

We walked all around and climbed the walls and explored different towers – all very well fortified. Within the town, the streets were small, narrow, and cobbled, with a central drain down each, and charming, as were the houses on either side. There were the usual spate of restaurants and antique and souvenir shops, but most houses were private dwellings. We lunched at a restaurant in an ancient square and listened to a strolling player. It was wonderful, and I'm so glad our family can have a taste of European life. After lunch, we walked through more of the town and saw the beautiful cathedral before coasting down the hill and back to the hotel. The towns here go to sleep between 12 and 2 p.m. but stay awake longer. Shops are open until 7 p.m., and the town really buzzes with activity until around 9 p.m.

September 13, without meaning to, we had chosen a hotel right next door to the marketplace, and, at 4 a.m. on Saturday, people were everywhere, setting up their stalls and wares. Outside our window was mainly clothes with live chickens and rabbits, etc. Beyond that, the butcher and cheaper shops were in the covered building to the right, and fruit, flowers, vegetables, nuts, and herbs down the street on an adjacent square.

After breakfast (Robin went out and bought fresh rolls and milk), the kids explored the market by themselves while we had a sleep-in. Robin then rode up to the airplane to repack it and plan for the next stage of the journey while I took the kids window shopping and did some clothes washing. We ate a fruit lunch when Robin returned and spent the afternoon playing down by the muddy river on the time- and weather-eroded rocks and walked back to the hotel for supper through beautiful gardens. I bought myself some good sunglasses, 84F, and a case, 7F. They are large and square and fun.

Rowena remembers:

These sunglasses were a key feature on Mum's face for the next twelve years, and I am sure connected her daily to this trip.

Nice
Carcassonne – Nice – 0.8 hrs. – IFR

Log notes:

Departed just in front of cold front. Passed through CU at 2,000 ft. Good VFR on top. Then descent through rain clouds to 1,500 ft. on ILS approach to Nice. Expensive landing fees.

Virginia's diary:

September 14, all set for our flight to Nice. We rode five km to the airport and had to hurry the usual pre-flight job of packing the plane, etc., because a cold front was quickly advancing over the area and could make it impossible for us to depart. The plane trip to Nice was very interesting because, as we passed over land from Carcassonne to the water, we saw old ruins on a high hill, plus peculiar-shaped fields radiating out like spokes from the centre – wedge-shaped – why this shape? We flew through some cloud and rain and finally came out into the open right over Marseilles, a large waterfront city. A short time after this, we were descending to the airport at Nice. It had nine shops right out on the water's edge. We flew down low over the water and could see the fabulous hotels along the edge, the gay sailing boats, and the sparkling water.

Figure 18 With the big guys at Nice.

We boarded the airport bus (no bikes this time) and rode to Place de Massena (centre of Nice). The road along by the waterfront was lined on one side by a wide promenade and the attractive grey cobblestone beach (where we can rent umbrellas, towels, etc., and swim) and on the other side the casino, larger hotels, and restaurants.

We consulted the green book and found that there are a number of hotels on Rue d'Angleterre and so walked there. We found Hotel Memblic Novelty, where we got a room with two doubles, one single, and breakfast for US$16. We went back down to the beach and played for a while. Robin then went off to find some supper and came back with Broinoski and my father (we had arranged to meet at American Express which was closed on Sunday but situated across the road).

Robin's Note:

Virginia's father, Robbie Stabb, was known by the kids as 'Man'. The Broinoskis were close friends and travelling companions of Robbie, who at the time was single, having recently divorced Virginia's mother, Wilga.

Stuart remembers:

We ate snails in shells in a good restaurant for the first time with Man and walked along the Nice promenade with Man and was impressed with all his stories about his trips around the world. We thought he sounded like he had the right idea about life – travel continuously! He also knew kids liked lots of ice cream, and he could do magic tricks with a handkerchief.

Virginia's diary:

Talked to Father a while. We ate our hot dogs and then all walked back to our respective hotels, which are situated quite close together, and arranged to meet at 10 a.m. the following day. Father looks very well and brown, and the kids loved to see him.

September 15, the sky today looked overcast, but it can't rain in Nice, so we didn't take our coats to Monaco! Unfortunately, the cold front proved us wrong, and, at about 12.15 p.m., the deluge started. However, we caught the train to Monaco and walked up the many steps to the palace just in time to see the changing of the guards in their white and red uniforms in front of the yellow ochre–coloured palace. The scene was so attractive, green palms and cactus all around and old green cannons and red and white sentry boxes. The crowd was large, so I do hope I managed to get a good picture of the scene.

Across the cobbled square from the palace, we went in search of lunch. The search included many winding, narrow streets and Italian-style stucco and plaster houses painted in delicate, sun-drenched pastel colours. We finally ended up by having wonderful hot dogs poked down the centre of slices of French bread, café au lait, and large soft ices in unusual flavours.

The rain was still pouring down, but we didn't mind. The scenery is so different and attractive. We followed the coastline around, walking on a garden cliff walk, hoping that it would bring us to see the luxurious collection of boats moored in the marina below. But we were too high above and so just had a distant view of them. They were lovely vessels, and there were two specially large, white, and beautiful ones – yachts. Caught the train back to Nice and said goodbye to Father. Back to the hotel for a late siesta and then we met again at 5.30 p.m. for drinks (red vino) with Father and the Broinoskis before we went home for our picnic supper.

Figure 19 Virginia and kids with Virginia's father, Robbie, at Nice.

September 16, met Father at 10 a.m. and said goodbye to the Broinoskis, who are travelling along towards Barcelona. Father will go with them when we depart on Friday for Rome. Decided to go for the day to Cimiez, a residential suburb on the hill behind Nice, where there are extensive Roman ruins (here was the ancient capital of Roman Gaul) set in magnificent gardens, an exquisite little museum of beautifully presented Roman artefacts on the ground floor, and a museum of Matisse on the first floor.

First we had rather a lengthy walk uphill and then purchased our lunch at some shops before the entrance gate to the gardens. Sat in the gardens and feasted and enjoyed an excellent bottle of rosé that Father had bought. Walked in the gardens and enjoyed the ruins and views of Naples harbour and mountains behind during siesta hours. The hill behind has four large telescopes (could see the domes), and a monastery was part of the gardens where we walked – loved the hot sun, vivid flowers, iron gates, and faded plaster. The ruins were quite extensive: one section seemed to be a round theatre with columns and archways around the exterior. The other seemed to be a collection of houses and streets. Robin could see where the houses had stood and showed me where some had supporting columns.

Next we walked to the museum (4F entrance for adults, declined to walk in the ruins for 1F fee). On the ground floor we saw many Etruscan exhibits of pottery, all lovely, mostly small bottles, plates, and lamps. Some were terracotta natural others were black painted, and others with black designs on them. We saw bone hair pins and jewellery. My favourites were a collection of tiny bronze figures 300–500 BC, all simple and modernistic in design and not more than four inches tall. The loveliest was a group of four women in a very simplified design.

We also saw how the Romans were buried in the ground with a tile roof placed longitudinally over the body, plus some stone and an iron coffin.

Upstairs was devoted to Matisse, a really exciting and unusual exhibit that even the kids appreciated. We saw his furniture, painting box and palettes, and also his many designs (progressing from sketches to the finished drawings) for the decoration of Chappelle Se Vence (twenty-five km on the road from Nice to Cannes). There were designs for stained glass windows, wall murals, and robes and surplices for the priest, all very new and modern. I wonder how they were first accepted. This work was done in the 1930s. His work at this stage is like Marimekko fabrics, vivid colours and forceful designs. We also saw two large silkscreen prints that were the designs for Aubusson tapestries of the sky and the sea.

After the museum, we walked down the hill (attractive large villas and apartments all around) aided by large ice creams that Dad bought for us and then back to our hotels for a brief siesta before we met at the bar near the station at 5.30 p.m. for a vino. The kids enjoyed the lemonade and were well behaved. Afterwards, a picnic in our rooms and to sleep.

September 17, met Father at 9.30 a.m. and walked to the Place de Massena where we caught an airport bus. Robin took the kids and my father up for a short flight (his first in a small aircraft) around Nice to Cannes and into the Alps behind. They returned at lunchtime (I sat in the airport and wrote the log), and we all caught the train to Cannes, had lunch (hot dog squeezed into a length of French bread, beer, and raisin juice), and set about looking at the marvellous selection of boats, many registered at Panama, that were moored at the marina. I have never seen such a large variety of luxury craft, both sail and power boats, and they looked fantastic under the brilliant sun, floating in shimmering water. We had ice cream to help hydration, for the day was very hot, and had a short siesta under some trees. Robin purchased Pan Brattan, gigantic rolls, for supper that were filled with lettuce, tomato, chopped onion, black olives, tuna, and liberal squirts of vinegar and olive oil. We washed that down with very good rosé wine and grapes supplied by Father and caught the train back to Nice in the early evening at 8 p.m.

Figure 20 On the beach at Cannes.

Cannes is similar to Nice except it has the marina and an attractive green belt of lawns and trees and brilliant flowers around the shore. The shops are very expensive and have beautiful quality clothes and furniture.

September 18, Father couldn't come with us today, as he had to deliver a suitcase to a friend. We decided we wanted to go to a beach and swim. Cap Ferrat was too far away from the train station, so we decided on Beaulieu Sur Mer instead, one stop past the stop to Cap Ferrat on the way to Villefranche. We purchased lunch at the supermarket and then walked past another large, fascinating marina full of international boats to the attractive but stony beach. The stones were small and white and the water a vivid blue, and so with the view of beautiful villas perched on the hillside behind us, we really felt that we were at the international playground. Shortly too, we became aware that this beach was definitely a topless one. It was interesting to hear the kids' comments while we sat on the rocks and ate our bread, salami, and cheese. The water was warm and very salty and delightful to swim in, so we stayed here until 3.30 p.m., when the sun became too hot, and then boarded a loaded train back to Nice.

Had a siesta – most necessary in this part of the world – and got ourselves ready for dinner with Father. He came and took the kids out to buy me some brilliant red carnations that were a tremendous treat and lovely to have in the bare hotel room. We all went to a restaurant nearby and drank red wine, ate wonderful jambon and champignon omelettes, shared six escargots, and had biscuits and camembert, and ice-cream sodas with café au lait to follow. It was a lovely meal and fun to hear of Father's experiences during his seven months in Europe and the United Kingdom. I'm so glad that we managed a rendezvous with him as it's something all six of us will always remember.

Southern Europe

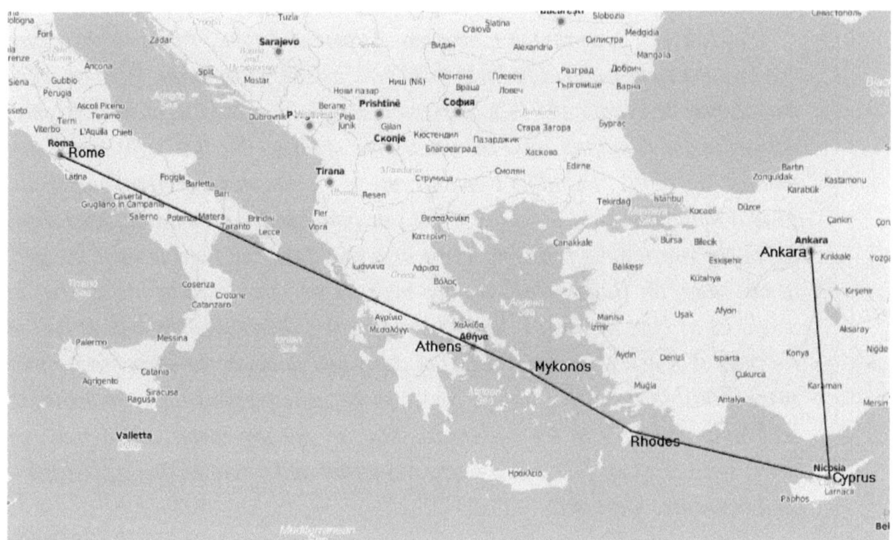

Figure 21 Southern Europe – Rome to Ankara.

Italy

Nice – Rome – 3.6 hrs. –VFR
Weather: haze on top

Log notes:

Italy – airport of entry – Roma. Flight: Nice–Rome (Ciampino). Decided to fly land route over Florence. Departed Nice 11 a.m. on departure 7 out to sea, then turned towards Genoa. Departure 7 reduces noise pollution over the city and provides the opportunity to climb to cruising of 10,000 ft. before reaching the mountains. Cleared to 12,000 ft., I needed some oxygen as we passed over the mountains. Good VFR day, scattered stratus. Straight in ILS to Rome – airport from five miles – Ciampino light aircraft, business and charter. Not Rome International.

Rome

Virginia's diary:

September 19, arrived at Ciampino Airport at 4 p.m., approximately (time one hr. later than Nice). The flight from Nice was very interesting. We flew along the coastline to Genoa and then overland to Rome. We could see numerous small villages in the mountains and the usual rows of vines. We flew right over Rome and all was visible, including Roman ruins in the surrounding green countryside. Had a roundabout but inexpensive bus ride into Roma Termini and, from there, began the search for a pensione. These at a good price are hard to come by, and, at one stage, an Italian took us on a walk to see some 'student' rooms that he would let us have at (two) US$19 per night. We didn't like the look of him or the place that was up a dozen flights of stairs and so began the boring search once more. Finished up with Pensione Stella at the same previous price, no breakfast and lousy plumbing in the bathrooms. Still, we got two rooms. At 8 p.m., we found some dried-up pizza at a pizza restaurant and ice cream and cappuccino – food expensive. Slept well.

September 20, awoke and breakfasted on croissants and soda that Robin had found in a tiny store below our pensione, coffee for me later. Walked to the Termini so that Robin could stand in a long line and get some lire, 660 = US$1. Then we walked through the streets of Roma (buying our coffee at a little shop on the way) towards the Coliseum. The latter is now open, and one is able to walk around inside it. Numerous tourist groups were there. It's all most impressive, most of the exterior marble facing had been removed long ago, but one can see the tiered seats and also the rooms below the area where slaves and wild animals were kept before the games. Unfortunately, Romans of today seem to have little respect for their treasures from ancient times as buildings are mercilessly defaced by graffiti and trash litters the ground. But, still, if one can forget these things, one can visualize the wonder and precision of the buildings as they once were.

Most were built of terracotta brick or huge chunks of stone and were faced with marble for decorative purposes. After seeing the Coliseum, we walked in a garden across the road. We saw about six brides and watched them along the street to the Coliseum.

The day was hot, and I had some bug, so we didn't stay long. Then we caught the underground at Colosseo to Termini and walked home for a siesta.

Dined that night on pizza again, but of a slightly superior quality, washed down with red vino and apple juice. Bathroom duty after supper for me as kids' heads needed to be washed, plus there was an accumulation of laundry.

September 21, decided today to catch a bus to the town of Tivoli, a half hour out in the country, to see the Villa d'Este, where there are five hundred fountains and Hadrian's Villa, which we did not see. However, we saw part of a young Communist rally and were able to stroll through the town, which was packed with tourist wares (Florentine trays, dolls, bags, mock marble statues of the Coliseum, backscratchers, inlaid boxes, and much, much more).

The Villa d'Este is a Renaissance villa, lovely inside with an attractive courtyard but, like most things in Italy, not cared for. We wondered why there was not a small admission charge that could pay for its' and the fountains' maintenance. Most of the fountains are working and are covered in green plants. It's very pretty. Water is used again and again as it drops down the hillside. There are very tall fountains, ones in caves that you can walk behind, long rows of small fountains, and many more. It was interesting to see such a beautiful and fascinating Renaissance way to pass time. We bought sandwiches and lots of local grapes for lunch and then walked around the town, looking down at the haze-shrouded countryside of Rome below us.

Caught the bumpy bus down to town again and, after a siesta, went out to a restaurant for a budget meal. We had tortellini (tiny different-shaped meatballs, like ravioli) with Bolognese sauce and parmesan, green salad, vino, and Fanta, plus delicious bread. Robin had an extra serve of lasagne. Meat doesn't seem to feature highly in Italian dishes; it is just sprinkled on pasta and never seen on pizza.

September 22, Angela has the bug today but follows bravely on. We ate breakfast at a stand-up coffee and croissant restaurant. The cappuccino and hot milk are excellent, and many people seem to breakfast at these places en route to work. We took the train to Colosseo and then walked to the Forum where we spent two-and-a-half hours at this political and religious centre of the ancient Romans. Marvelled at the number of temples (felt sorry for the Vestal Virgins), the size of the columns, the craftsmanship to be seen in the stone carvings, and the clever engineering of hot-air ducts and sewerage (we think) tunnels under the whole thing. From the look, and from what is still standing, we could gain a clear picture of what it was like, and we found it fun to use our imaginations to think of what life would be like for us then.

After a lunch of hot dogs, hamburgers, and Pepsi for fortification, we set out to walk across Rome to the Pantheon. This is a huge temple. Inside, it is faced with many different kinds and colours of marble. Also, there are different religious booths and a coin-in-the-slot taped description (plus TV film for 100 lire) of the Pantheon. What Robin and I found most interesting was the ceiling – a huge dome, patterned in squares, and once faced with bronze (the bronze was removed and later used in the construction of St Peter's). In the centre of the dome was a large aperture, nine ft. in diameter and open to the sky. We wondered what happens when it rains and then noticed small holes at varying intervals in the slightly dipped marble floor where water would drain and be mopped into drains below the ground floor.

Outside, we sat by a Rameses II needle and ate delicious gelati. It was around 2.45 p.m. in Rome. All shops were closed, all restaurants open and doing a good trade, and all streets quiet (shops and businesses close from 1–4 p.m.). Next we walked to the Trevi fountain, past several old buildings with delightful interior courtyards and gardens. One particularly pleasing courtyard doubled as a repository for marble and bronze statues and as a car park. Found we were footsore at Trevi fountain and so took off our shoes and soaked our feet in the cold water. There are many tourists here, and it is pretty.

After this, we walked to the Via Vittoria Veneto. We didn't see many luscious shops but managed to purchase two wallets for the mothers and saw the usual huge US embassy with armed guards outside and another subway station in the process of being built.

Rome's subway was commenced fifty years ago and still consists of ten stations in a straight line. Excavation and building can only proceed at inches each year because of Roman ruins that stand in the way.

Bought delicious ham, ricotta, bread, and grapes for supper in our hotel room and went out for cappuccino afterwards.

Greece

Rome – Athens – 4.9 hrs –mostly VFR
Weather: some turbulence, strong winds

Log note:

Departure delayed till two o'clock because of BP lousy service and installing the thirty-gallon aux. tank. Climb out around early afternoon cumulus clouds before setting course en route. Good VFR. On top all the way. Some bumps. Descent into Athens. RW 33, very turbulent with strong winds – landing just after sunset.

Caught taxi from airport to hotel. Customs good at airport with 24-hour money changing. Aircraft parked right in front of new international terminal. No landing or parking fees. Accommodation arranged by private company at airport. Good C-class hotel – two rooms with showers and breakfasts for 540 DR (US$18) per day at Hotel Theoexonia, behind Omonia Square, Gastonos Street.

Virginia's diary:

September 23, rose early, having packed the night before, and were all on our way having cappuccino and croissants by 8.30 a.m. Unfortunately, missed the 8.40 bus to Ciampino airport and not another one till 10 a.m. Robin fumed but was able to send a telegram to Turkey during the intervening time. Finally, our bus arrived, and we were on our bumpy (Fiat buses are lousy, both space and comfort-wise) to the airport. We repacked and placed the auxiliary tank (which we had filled here to test its usability en route to Athens) and, at 1.45 p.m. took off for Athens, flying across Italy to Brindisi and then across a small stretch of water to Greece. The weather was good all the way and flying at 11,000 ft.

Athens

Robin remembers:

September 24 – The family rested in our hotel room most of the day while I caught a bus to the airport (21dr) to check out the route from Athens to Ankara. There is only one route open, and that is via Rhodes, Cypress, and then directly north to Ankara. I decided to re-fuel at Rhodes, then non-stop to Ankara, with Cypress as alternative. I returned to hotel in better spirits and found the family well after rest and a lunch of small kebabs and ice cream. For supper, we had more kebabs followed by light Greek pastries with almond filling and sugar and cinnamon (✓✓✓✓✓), all bought from fast-food counters in two arcades.

Virginia's diary:

September 25, after a continental breakfast in the hotel, we walked (walk took one-and-a-half hours) through the city and Plaka district where could be seen numerous Greek arts and crafts shops containing hand-woven rugs, garments and cotton women's clothing, brass and copper dishes and ornaments, wool sweaters and rugs, copies of ancient pottery, and jewellery of the more traditional and hippy kind (beads, etc.). We bought lunch on the way and found ourselves going through steeper and narrower whitewashed streets. We followed hand-painted signs to the Acropolis. It's rocky up on the top. The vegetation is sparse, and the rocks all shine with constant usage. We encountered some tourist buses, bought a guidebook explaining the ancient ruins of Athens, and then entered the Acropolis through the main gate of the Propylaea: like the other buildings, it was first built as a place of worship and of cultural and government exchange but later used by the Turks (Byzantine period) as a storage place for munitions. The classical perfection of these ruins against the clear blue Aegean sky is most stirring.

Figure 22 At the Parthenon.

We visited the Parthenon (unable to go inside), and all around us on the Acropolis were old fragments of carved stone that had been broken from the buildings. The kids were intrigued by inscriptions they saw and by broken carvings. They were also pleased because they could climb where they liked and discovered holes in the ground and old tunnels (probably old sewerage). We also visited the Acropolis museum and saw fragments of very early sculpture that had been broken off by early plunderers and then used to make a wall to fortify the Acropolis against a Turkish invasion; luckily, it was safe from further plundering and only recently had been removed to the museum. It seemed clear to us that Greeks are rather against the English for plundering so much of the stone on the Acropolis. Then in the eighteenth century, much of one side of the Parthenon and one of the virgins were removed to a specially prepared museum in London.

We had rather a luscious brunch. What Robin had thought were sausage rolls turned out to be rich moist pastries filled with a spicy, cinnamon-type of cake (baklava). We had grapes and Pepsi too.

About 2.30 p.m., we went down around the Acropolis, passing two open-air theatres. One was Roman, constructed during Roman occupation, now restored and in use today; the second, an older Greek one, now in ruins, was more interesting because we could see the seating for important guests plus the interesting carvings that marked the back of the stage. From here, we walked a little more and came upon the excavations of two Byzantine cisterns (sewerage?), both in good repair, saw some ruins – unrecognizable except for a hostelry with horse troughs nearby – and then out into the street and back to the hotel. For supper that night, Robin and I tried moussaka (20dr each) and the kids had a hamburger with egg on top and chips. Slept well and feeling great.

September 26, decided today to walk to the Ancient Agora and Temple Hephaestus. We walked there by way of the markets. The varieties of fish, squid, octopus, mussels, and shrimp were fantastic. we also saw many kinds of cheeses and meats. We purchased lunch and ate it in a park before we went to the Temple Hephaestus (god of arts and crafts). This is one of the better preserved ruins. On the walls are graffiti and names of tourists, dating way back to the sixteenth century, plus an epithet by Byron to a friend who is buried there. This temple is set amongst gardens, lawns, and pomegranate trees and is really beautiful.

We walked down the hill then to see old Greek ruins of pottery works and of a local town meeting place where news was posted. There are also ruins of shops and homes. To the left of us, on a lower level by the railway line, were some pre-Hellenic ruins that we did not look at. The Ancient Agora was a marketplace and assembly, completely restored in its original style by the American School of Classical Studies in Athens. It now houses a rare (museum) collection of clay pots that shows the evolution of design and various articles dug up from nearby graves. It was all very fascinating as we were able to see examples from different periods of pottery – Dozer (Rowena) found a child's commode.

We then walked home in the heat of the day in time to have a siesta before supper. This time it was kebabs again; lush pastries, our favourite kind; and a walk around Omonia Square before home to bed.

Athens – Mykonos – 1.0 hr. – VFR

September 27, this morning we boarded a taxi for the airport and then Robin flew us an hour SE of Athens to the island of Mykonos where we planned to spend three days of beaching. Mykonos is a small barren island with a town of the same name, just three km (we walked) from the airport. The scenery is interesting, lots of small white square, flat-roofed houses, some cacti, narrow roads, and the occasional donkey ambling along. All very peaceful and serene and always not too far away the marvellous blue of the Mediterranean.

Mykonos

When we arrived at the town, we found it was a maze of tiny narrow streets, all cobbled and different levels, and it was impossible to find the pension that we had an address for. Luckily, a woman asked us if we needed rooms (this seems to be the way that many of the islanders earn their living), and so we decided to look at what she offered. It turned out to be no palace but OK accommodation – five beds and a bathroom in two rooms, no breakfast, for $10 per night. We then went for a walk along the seashore and noticed that the town becomes alive at night. White buildings suddenly became shops that have their wares displayed outdoors or restaurants that emit marvellous cooking smells. Along the waterfront are several bars, and it was here that we decided to try a bottle of local white wine – very good.

We dined on oily but tasty moussaka, a combination of eggplant and minced lamb topped by mashed potato mixed with feta. Before this though, we found an old working windmill (the only working one out of five) and were asked by the miller to climb up and see what was happening. It was fun for us all to see the internal workings of the old mill, all floury and grinding way.

September 28, bought pastries at the bakery shop and ate with coffee before boarding the 10.30 a.m. bus to Ornos Beach, a 5dr ride about twenty minutes from Mykonos. Spent a lovely, lazy day swimming and tanning. The sand was not fine but reasonable, water blue, and inviting temperature. The kids found a wrecked boat and played in it very happily. There were two or three restaurants at the edge of beach where some of the people on the beach ate leisurely lunches, but we had brought five cheese doughboys (boiled dumpling) and so were satisfied. We really enjoyed ourselves here and caught the 4.30 p.m. bus home. Ate shish kebabs and ice cream and walked in the streets at suppertime – town most colourful. Stuart was rather unwell because of sunstroke, but better the next day.

Figure 23 On the beach at Mykonos.

September 29, another lazy day, the Frith beachcombers went by bus to Plati Yild today for a further dose of Mediterranean sun. We took along watermelon and grapes and added ice cream for lunch, and everyone felt that sun prevents hunger developing at noon. By mid-afternoon we decided to walk along a narrow cliff path to Paradise Beach (where a boat will transport one for an extra 10dr) to see what it could offer. The beach was not impressive, but nude swimmers and sunbathers provided the different feature in the landscape. All around here the blue sky and turquoise sea contrast beautifully with the stark rocky landscape and little white buildings.

Figure 24 Shopping in Mykonos.

Dined again at Spiros and had memorable souvlaki (kebabs) pork and lemon juice seasoned with thyme, we think. Had tomato, cucumber salads garnished with parsley and black olives, island bread, and red wine. Slept well.

September 30, after a late, late start (because of noisy Germans departing about 6 a.m. and asking all their beachcombing friends in for early morning showers) we went to the bank and then by bus to Ornos Beach again. The beach was practically deserted, and the kids immediately set to on their boat. Robin did a mammoth swim, and we had lots of honeydew melon and ice cream for lunch.

We returned to Mykonos (village) at 4.30 p.m. Had toasted egg and bacon sandwiches, fresh tomatoes, and large hunks of spice cake for supper. There was a big wash that night for me, and it hung by the blue line (dripping occasionally) over Robin's and my beds.

Turkey

Mykonos – Rhodes – Ankara – 2.0 + 6.0 hrs – IFR Ankara

October 1, up at 6.30 a.m. and travelled out to Mykonos airport by taxi. We are off in the airplane by 8.30 a.m. We arrived in Rhodes and bought cardboard sandwiches and drinks for lunch. Robin filed the flight plan to Ankara (via Cyprus) and got the aircraft refuelled. We departed for Ankara at 11.30 a.m. for the six-hour flight.

Robin remembers:

The filing of a flight plan from Greece to Turkey was not as straightforward as Virginia's diary implies. At the time of this flight, there was a war going on between Greece and Turkey, over Cyprus. When I approached flight service to file the flight plan from Rhodes to Ankara, the flight service attendant asked 'Where?' when I mentioned Ankara. He supposedly had not heard of it and would not accept it as a destination from Greece.

As there was no way we could fly through the Middle East at that time (Israel, Egypt, and Lebanon were at war), some quick thinking on my part was called for, and so I filed two flight plans: Rhodes–Beirut then Beirut–Ankara. This was acceptable, so we departed Rhodes, bound for Beirut, then, over the top of Cyprus, cancelled the Beirut flight plan by radio with the Greek flight controllers and picked up the Ankara flight plan with the Turkish controllers. We turned left and headed for Ankara.

Virginia's diary:

October 1, flew around Cyprus so as to avoid Nicosia, went across a small stretch of water, and soon sighted and were flying over Turkey. High peaks gave way to desert-like scenery below us, and, at 12,000 ft., hardly any green vegetation could be seen. We flew over some villages in desert areas and a few lucky ones that were situated near water supplies so agriculture could take place and shade trees could grow.

Reached Ankara at 5 p.m., after six hours from Rhodes. We were met by Emil of Celebi, our designated agent, who directed us to his office, booked rooms at Stad Oteli, and ushered us into a taxi. About a half hour's ride from the airport, Ankara started to appear. First, on barren hillsides, we saw thousands of 'jerry-built' houses, some not connected with electricity or sewerage. Occupants of these dwellings have come from outlying villages to seek work at Ankara and are allowed free land on the hills. The houses are mainly constructed at election time when there is general confusion politically and it's easy to evade the law.

Ankara is a seething mass of people. Turkey's population has grown from fourteen million to forty million in recent years (2007, seventy million).

Apartments are everywhere. Turkey does not have a reliable yearly rainfall, and its climate is cold and dry.

We had sausage meat and chips and salad for dinner at the hotel and then dropped exhausted into our beds.

Rowena recalls:

I had a very unpleasant experience in Ankara. When being shown to our room in the hotel, the bellboy illustrated the fact that the room had hot water by grabbing my hand and placing it under the running water. It was not just hot; it was boiling and burnt my hand severely!

October 2, the beginning of a most frustrating day. First we discovered that our Iranian visas (due to an error of ours) were invalid and so had to get new photos taken and leave passports at the Iranian embassy. Much time was taken up by phone calls about the latter and also to try and determine where we could refill our oxygen cylinder. At 3 p.m. we took a taxi to KOC oxygen factory, but they didn't have the right fitting for our cylinder. So we are going to have to make the next flight with 60 per cent oxygen left.

Passports should be ready on Saturday morning at 1 p.m., and so we'll have to spend another day in Ankara. Robin took the kids for a short walk in an amusement park opposite the hotel and then we all decided to have supper there. We found a cheap restaurant and had difficulty in ordering (menu in Turkish) but finished up with tasty pizza, salads, and yoghurt-type milk for the kids (the latter was an unsuccessful purchase as they didn't like it).

We seemed to create interest in the café, and soon a young man called Hamet, who said he was a student at the University in necrology, a new field, joined us. (Necrology: a list or record of people who have died, especially in the recent past.) We talked for quite a long while. His English was much better than our Turkish, and he gave Stuart his leather armband and Robin his metal key ring. We exchanged addresses, so maybe he will call on us in Sydney one day.

Robin sent a telegram to Iran to advise authorities that we were on our way.

October 3, after breakfast, went to the post office and sent two more telegrams: one to reserve rooms in Teheran, and one to Karachi to advise the airport that we were coming. We also posted postcards. Then walked along the main boulevard into the busy commercial area of the city.

Not an attractive (because it's grown so quickly, I suspect) but a very busy city. We bought some lunch, looked at shops in arcades, and then walked home. Spent from 2–6 p.m. in the hotel room, resting and washing hairs. Then spent one hour enjoying half a bottle of Turkish red wine while the kids played cards. Dined at 7 p.m. from a fixed price menu – 26 lira for three-course meal: soup or salad, casserole of meat (veal) and vegetables, and fruit salad. The kids loved this. And then bed.

Turkey to Australia

The Home Stretch

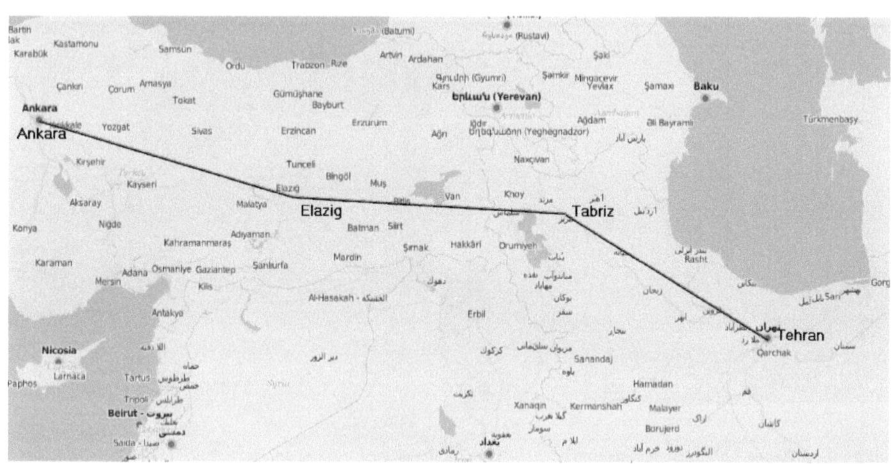

Figure 25 Ankara to Tehran.

Ankara – Elazig – 2.6 hrs – VFR

October 4, up, breakfasted, packed, and out of hotel by 9.15 a.m. We took a taxi to the Iranian embassy, and we were in luck as the visas were ready (they had been stamped on the second!), and so we took the same taxi to airport. We sat in Emil's office while Robin filed the flight plan, refuelled, etc., and then took off at 11.05 a.m. for Elazig, a flight of two-and-a-half hours.

We are now flying now at 11,500 ft. The countryside below is similar to what we saw on our way to Ankara. The ground in some areas is tilled, so cultivation of it must take place, perhaps in spring and summer. But now it's fall, and the ground below us is for the most part colourless.

Elazig

We arrived at Elazig at 4 p.m. local time and took a taxi to the centre. The airport must have been a US air force base in the '50s. It is very Turkish and perhaps difficult for us to get used to. All the older buildings are of mud and daub, sometimes covered in a thin layer of cement, and new buildings are of a hollow ceramic brick. Elazig is noisy, smelly, and dirty. Our hotel is smelly too but the only one available.

Figure 26 On the tarmac in Elazig.

Angela remembers:

This was our first trough toilet and washing yourself with a sponge on the end of the stick. Yuck! We wondered how people stayed clean. Breakfast at the hotel was starting to have different flavours. Everything looked the same but tasted different. This included rose-petal jam that looked like strawberry jam and goat's cheese that looked like butter.

Virginia's diary:

Turkish toilet facilities are different: there is no sit-down lavatory, just a place where one crouches, and also no toilet paper is provided. However, one gets used to this. Dinner was interesting, a tray of cold hors d'oeuvres, e.g., liver in olive oil, olives, salads, beans, etc., (6TL each) before rice and shish kebabs with watermelon or grapes for dessert. We were lulled to sleep by Eastern music from the streets below, but at 1 a.m. we were awakened by a man walking along the road and banging a gong to proclaim the beginning of a Muslim holiday. The Iranians' five-day holiday started two days later, and it corresponds to our Christmas, so I imagine the Turkish holiday is for the same thing.

Iran

Elazig – Tehran – 5.1 hrs. – VFR

October 5, breakfast was at 7 a.m. as we hoped to depart for Tehran, five-and-a-quarter hours away at 8.30 a.m. The meal was unusual. Black tea for everyone, served in glasses, fresh white bread, butter, goat's milk cheese, and rose-petal jam. The kids weren't sure about the cheese and jam but said it was okay and now love black tea.

The flight to Tehran was a lonely one for Robin but also provided him with a great sense of achievement because of the ruggedness of the terrain that he had to fly through. He climbed to 13,000 ft. and used oxygen when he needed it. As we couldn't refill the cylinder at Ankara, the kids and I could not use it.

We flew over some peaks and passed by others and had magnificent view of the most extraordinary scenery that one could imagine. We saw tiny villages (mud and daub dwellings with flat roofs nestling anywhere that there was a patch of green to be seen). These villages were often very tiny and extremely isolated (we wondered what kind of life the people led).

We flew past high snow-covered peaks, strange and colourful rock formations, large lakes (on different levels) with no sign of human habitation around them, and all during the five-and-a-quarter hours never spotted another plane. At one stage, Robin was talking to a Russian Aeroflot captain (pilot) who gave him Tehran's weather as neither of them could make radio contact with Tehran. Most of the time, radio contact was excellent, however, and kids were fascinated by all that they saw in this beautiful and wild country.

Figure 27 Turkish mountains.

Robin recalls:

The leg from Elazig to Tehran was one of the most spectacular and challenging of the whole trip. Having been unable to re-fill the oxygen cylinder in Ankara, I had no choice, with the projected flying altitudes of up to 14,000 feet, but to reserve the remaining oxygen for the pilot.

I felt bad about this as the kids felt that I may have put Virginia and their lives at risk by flying at a high altitude with low oxygen levels, but in reality, the only risk was mild hypoxia (light-headedness) as the exposure to high altitude was of a very limited duration. It was not as if they were exerting themselves by climbing a mountain at this altitude.

Elazig Airport is at around 3,000 ft. above sea level, and, on take-off, we climbed to 13,000 ft. and set course for Tehran.

Virginia describes very well the rugged terrain below en route, but I was fascinated by the sights of Lake Van at 6,500 ft. above sea level, off to our left and a line of volcanic mountains bordering the north shore of Lake Van: Nemrut Dagi at 10,000 ft.; Suphan Dagi at 13,720 ft.; and Tendurak Dagi at 11,800 ft.

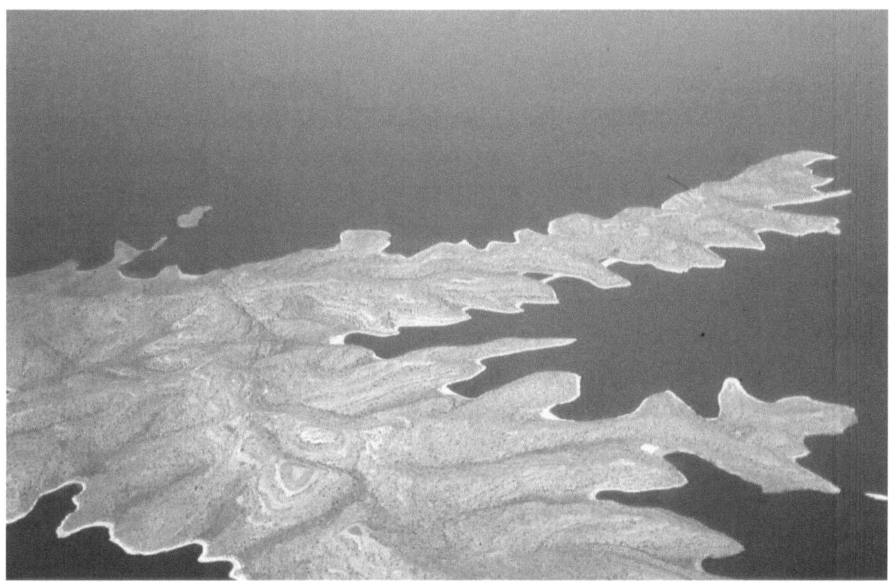

Figure 28 The desolate shore of Lake Van.

As we flew over Nemrut Dagi, which last erupted in AD 1441, we could look down into the perfectly formed circular rim of the crater.

In the distance to the left, we could see the Black Sea, then the Soviet States of Georgia, Armenia, and Azerbaijan as we passed over the city of Tabriz (second-largest city in Iran in 1975) as we entered Iranian air space. It is amazing the visibility you have from 14,000 ft. with the clear blue skies and absolutely no air pollution in this area.

Off to our right was the snow-capped peak of the extinct Sahand Volcano (12,200 ft.) and further to our left towards the Caspian Sea the snow- and glacier-covered volcano of Sabalan (also extinct), the second-highest mountain in Iran.

From Tabriz, we then flew in a direct line to Tehran with the Elburz Mountain range bordering the southern edge of the Caspian Sea with peaks up to 12,000 ft. off to the left, between us and the Caspian Sea.

As we descended to land in Tehran, the highest peak in Iran, the snow-capped Mount Damarand (18,700 ft.) thirty miles to the north-east, was quite spectacular.

Tehran

Tehran came upon us suddenly, a huge bustling city with a high mountain (18,000 ft.) behind it and, like Ankara, busily trying to shake off feudal ways and enter the twentieth century way of life (this is true of the whole country). Therefore, it is a city of contrasts, large modern buildings on streets with sometimes unfinished sidewalks. Cars are everywhere, and drivers are fast and aggressive. There is much effort to build public gardens and plant trees by roadsides. The people are a contrast also; many women are veiled in black and floral cotton material, but underneath the floor-length veil one sees a fashionable dress or a tight pair of jeans. Street hawkers are everywhere: fruit, vegetables, cloths, books – you name it, you'll find it. At 7 p.m., Robin *saw a little boy of about eleven sitting on the sidewalk doing his homework for school and all set up with scales to weigh passers-by for a small charge; another common occupation for young boys and old men is shoe cleaning, but still one sees this in Italy and Greece also.*

For our first night in Tehran, we stayed at Hotel Golden Star – not recommended ($25 with breakfast) – situated in the bottom centre part of town in a rather slummy area. The hotel is dirty and smelly and noisy with Indian families staying there. However, we were provided with a filling hot dinner for only $1.50 each, spicy chicken and rice (saffron and sultanas in rice), unleavened bread, Fanta, and a nice-looking salad that we could not possibly eat because the dressing on it smelt and tasted like perfume and methylated spirits mixed.

Angela remembers:

Teheran seemed very primitive in parts, but, in contrast, there were cars, a freeway infrastructure, and, of course, TVs and an airport. The things that seemed primitive included: donkeys and carts in the street. In the Persian carpet shop, there were whole rooms of women weaving carpets in dark rooms. We were told they were blind because they had spent their whole lives in these rooms.

Virginia's diary:

October 6, we moved from this hotel after breakfast (goat's milk cheese, unleavened bread, butter, fig jams, and black tea – nice) and commenced to look for somewhere suitable to spend the night (somewhere without a smell). Hotel Cashier filled the bill and provided us with two rooms (Persian carpets on the floor), bathroom, and breakfast for $40. It was also near the Australian embassy, US embassy, and the post office. We seemed to spend a lot of time that day at embassies, trying to find out where a Burmese *consulate is in India and sending a telegram to airport authorities in Karachi to let them know that we were coming.*

Beautiful antiques and rugs and handicrafts are available in Tehran: my favourites are the brass or copper or silver samovars (tea urns) and the silver and turquoise jewellery and cigarette boxes, but all are far too highly priced for us. Instead, I found some old hand-carved wood blocks once used for fabric printing. They have exquisite designs on them, and I plan to hang them in a group on a wall and also to use them to print Christmas cards. We bought six for around $70.

We also spent some time inside a carpet shop looking at Persian carpets. Mostly they were silk ones of intricate design and delicate colouring. They were large and were selling for $15,000–$25,000 each! We also saw one in the process of being woven by two young men. The carpet was strung between two rollers against a wall, and the men sat on scaffolding five ft. from floor level working on it.

Back to the hotel's snack bar for supper, omelettes, eggs and bacon, and a beer for us and an early night before the long flight to Zahedan.

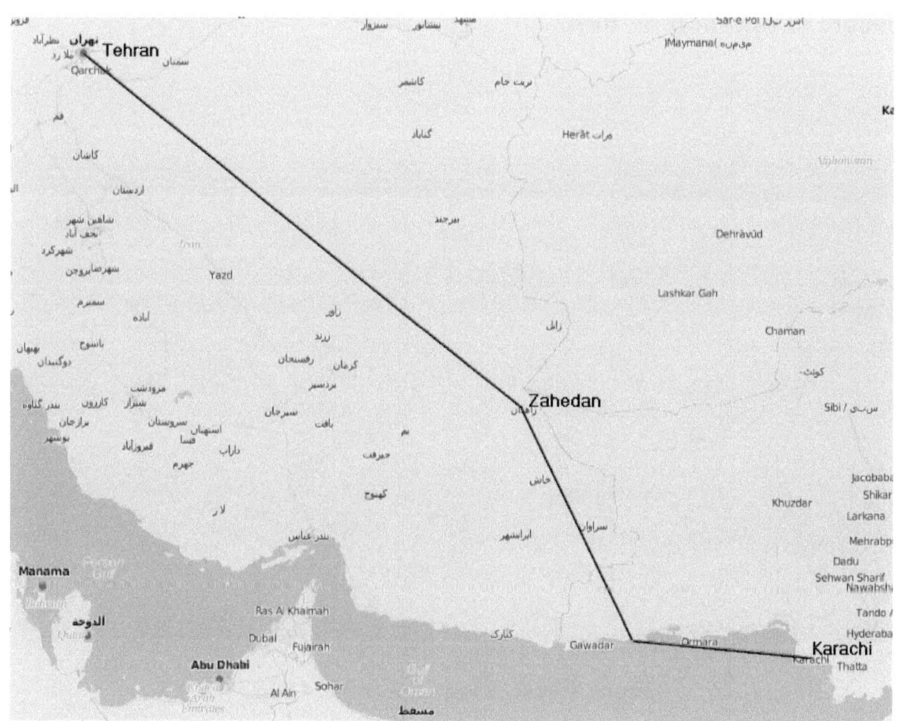

Figure 29 Tehran to Zahedan is six hours over desert.

Tehran – Zahedan – 6.0 hrs. – VFR

From Tehran, our next major stop was to be Karachi, Pakistan, but as neither our human nor aircraft endurance would stretch that far, we decided to break the journey at the only substantial town with an international airport in south-eastern Iran, Zahedan.

Zahedan is located close to the junction of the borders with Afghanistan and Pakistan, an area best known in 2010 as the centre of the Western democracy's battle with the Taliban and al-Qaida.

To get from Tehran to Zahedan involved a 1,000-mile (1,620-km) flight across some of the most inhospitable and uninhabited areas of the world – the Dasht-e Kavir (Great Salt Desert) and the Dasht-e Lut (Emptiness Desert).

Virginia describes it best in her log, but from the time we departed Tehran and climbed to our cruising altitude of 10,000 ft. (5,000 ft. about the ground) it was sandy desert, salt plains, and rocky ranges right up to Zahedan on the edge of the desert.

Not the sort of country where you would want to have an engine failure or run short on fuel!

Figure 30 Flying across the Great Salt Desert.

October 7, up early today and out at the airport by 8.45 a.m., but it was 11.30 a.m. before Robin got through briefing and meteorology because of language difficulties and because not many privately owned aircraft fly out from here. However, I spent an hour having an interesting conversation with an Iranian guy who wants to go to California to study medicine, so time went quickly.

It took a further half hour to get from the transit lounge through passport clearance and out to the plane – FRUSTRATIONS – because at each doorway there was a policeman who barred our way and could not understand our reason for wanting to go through.

We flew entirely through desert for six hours to Zahedan. We passed by a few small settlements (one by the radio beacon) that were situated mainly at the base of hills. The movement of the winds in the dust and sand had created fabulous patterns, deep whorls and gullies to look down upon. At one time, it looked just like a frosted cake and at another like a movie set for Lawrence of Arabia.

Visibility was good at one hundred miles, but there was quite a noticeable haze.

Zahedan

Zahedan is a prosperous town of seventy thousand[9] *persons, and we landed there at 4 p.m. It was hot outside, and a warm dry wind was blowing. We are trying to find out what industry is at Zahedan, a town right in the middle of the desert, for lots of construction is going on. The airport manager took us by jeep to Zahedan Inn, a comfortable place where we had a beer and met three English truck drivers (one from Aldershot, London, and two from Stoke-on-Trent) and talked.*

Stuart remembers:

The English truck drivers gave us their hats and gave me a leather bracelet. We had to walk three miles in the desert heat.

Virginia's diary:

They had driven large semi-trailers from England through Europe (taken 17–25 days) to Iran with road construction equipment on board for a new highway. In the bar and lounge, we saw lots of workers, some Australians, one who said this is an asshole of a place: working conditions must be difficult. We

---

[9] The population had grown to six hundred thousand by 2001.

did not drive into the town but saw it from the air the next day – many small buildings, haciendas, with half-circle roofs seemed to denote that lots of single men live here. We had good supper and breakfast and felt refreshed the following day but discovered that because I'd had two vermouths the night before we had no taxi money left and needed to walk to the airport.

Pakistan

Zahedan – Karachi – 3.5 hrs. – VFR

We departed Zahedan in clear, calm conditions and were immediately over desert again as we headed south towards the Gulf of Oman and Arabian Sea.

With very limited radio navigation aids available in this area, my strategy was to follow the Iran–Pakistan border on a south, south-east course until I hit the coast of the Arabian Sea and then turn to the east and follow the coast to Karachi.

Figure 31 The unique mountain range formation of the Iran–Pakistan border.

Out of Zahedan, the desert landscape soon gave way to mountain ranges up to 10,000 ft. with very distinctive geologic folds as we passed over the Central Makran Range in Pakistan and then across the twenty-mile-wide coastal plains bordering the Arabian Sea.

Once we hit the coast, with clear skies, we were able to follow the coast to a landing at Karachi International Airport.

October 8, departed Zahedan at 11 a.m. on three-and-a-half-hour flight to Karachi. Weather is hot and good. We flew over desert for the first two hours until well into Pakistan when we began to fly over curious and very unusual rock formations, lots of faults, and deep canyons. There are very few villages here still, and very little green seen from the aircraft at 11,000 and 12,000 ft. Rocks gave way to sand once more as we flew along the coastline (Arabian Sea) towards Karachi. Landed at Karachi airport at 4 p.m. and went through customs and then walked to Midway House, the old KLM motel where Robin and I had stayed eleven years previously. We dined at the snack bar on soup, spicy beef, and fruit salad and dropped into bed.

Karachi

October 9, Robin contacted the helpful Australian consul in Karachi who has sent a telex to Calcutta. Hopefully we can get a Burmese visa there. We had a rest day, so we located the swimming pool after breakfast and spent most of the day beside it. There was a small Dozer- (Rowena-) sized pool alongside the large one, and she demonstrated how well she could do the prone float. Stuart took the plunge and jumped off the high-diving board. We had ice cream by the pool and then ate dinner in the restaurant – quite a delectable Mexican steak, soup, and fruit salad for $2.00 per head.

India

Karachi – Ahmadabad – 2.8 hrs. –VFR

The next leg of our journey was a short flight from Karachi, Pakistan, to Ahmadabad, India. Ahmadabad was the designated port of entry into India, so we could look forward to all the bureaucracy associated with customs and immigration procedures in India.

On take off, we headed south-east and were soon passing over the estuary of the mighty Indus River – originating in the Tibetan plateau and flowing south along the length of Pakistan for 3,200 km (2 000 miles) before emptying into the Arabian Sea.

The very extensive low-lying silt deposits at the mouth of the river were obvious to us in the aircraft, as were the salt marshes and sandy scrub of the Rann of Kutch as we moved on to Ahmadabad.

As we approached Ahmadabad, the marshes gave way to agricultural land under crops. The kids were fascinated by the tiny plots of land that constituted farms that produced meagre incomes for the farming families.

Figure 32 Subsistence farming approaching Ahmedabad.

October 10, Robin decided on a late start today for Ahmadabad, and we wanted to wait and see if there were any telexes in for us from Calcutta (no luck) and also give the kids another swim. At 11.20, we departed the airport for Ahmadabad, a three-hour flight away. We flew across flood plains and intensely cultivated and very green areas and past many small villages that looked most attractive from 10,000 ft.

Ahmadabad[10]

The frustrating part commenced at 4 p.m. when we landed at the small and 'down-at-heel' airport at Ahmadabad. It took two hours for Robin to get us through customs (and we had to empty all our bags). In immigration and air traffic control, Robin had to fill out dozens of useless forms and had to make two copies of the same two forms at each of the three places. Finally, the immigration man forgot to stamp one of the forms, and we had to come and do it the next morning, thus delaying our departure further (it took two hours to take-off too). What tickled me: the special forms Robin had to fill out so that the customs man could be paid overtime that night and Saturday morning and that he was convinced we needed customs clearance to depart Ahmadabad, even though we were just going to Nagpur; the four men that rode with the doctor in the jeep just to spray one little can of disinfectant into the airplane; the fact that after all of this fuss no one asked to see our health cards; and the place seems bogged down by paperwork and everyone has an offsider to help, even when there is no work to do.

We stayed at the Cama Hotel, which was comfortable and had air conditioning, though the food was of poor quality.

---

[10] On 26 January 2001, a devastating earthquake centered near Bhuj, measuring 6.9 on the Richter scale, struck the city. As many as fifty multi-storied buildings collapsed, killing 752 people. More than 20,000 people were killed in the total Kutch areas affected by the quake.

Ahmadabad – Nagpur – 3.3 hrs. – VFR

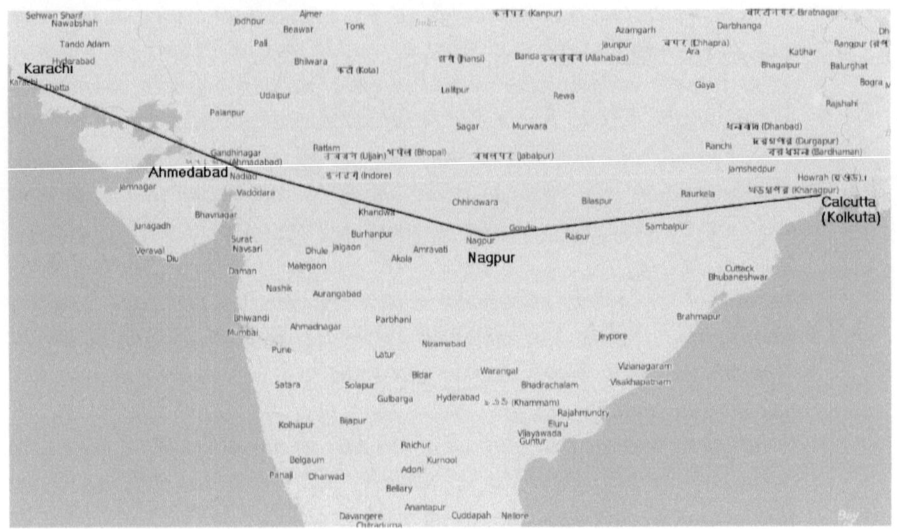

Figure 33 Ahmadabad, Nagpur, and Calcutta.

There was no particular reason for stopping at Nagpur other than to re-fuel and re-fresh. Nagpur is at the geographic centre of the Indian landmass and was a medium-sized city when we visited. The flight from Ahmadabad to Nagpur was uneventful, with no distinguishing landmarks along the route, and fine weather for the whole of the trip.

> *October 11, arrived at the airport at 9 a.m. and departed two hours later for Nagpur. Flying at 11,500 ft. over central India. The land is very flat and, for the most part, highly cultivated and green. There are some small forest areas and many villages with tiled roofs. We arrived at 3 p.m., and, after seeing the customs man and buying a fresh lime drink (very hot weather), we drove into Nagpur.*

Nagpur

> *Now we are in Central India, and the countryside looks good from a distance but close up one can notice poverty in the number of sub-standard dwellings along the road. Nagpur, at 5 p.m., is a crowded city full of people, many bicycles and pedicabs, and a few cars, most of them taxis. It is dirty, dusty, and smelly with few good-quality buildings. The marketplace is*

colourful and so are all the women in their bright-coloured saris. We saw a body on the way to the cemetery. It was lying on a flower-bedecked stretcher that was carried by four sons (the dead person's children, presumably).

After looking at two hotels, we decided upon the Skylark, reputedly the best in town – $15 for two rooms and $9 for an excellent dinner of vegetable soup, Chinese chop suey, and ice cream (pasta and strawberry). The rooms were OK but without any frills and an air conditioner that worked intermittently. Everyone slept well, and we did not explore the town as we felt that there would be nothing gained by doing so.

Rowena remembers:

This was another unpleasant experience. As a five-year-old with very blonde hair, I was a source of curiosity for the black-haired Indian population. As I walked along, men would come up to me and run their fingers through my hair to feel its texture. This is very disconcerting when you are very young.

Nagpur – Calcutta (Kolkata) – 4.2 hrs. – VFR

Virginia's diary:

October 12, up early and breakfast of hard-boiled eggs, toast triangles, hot chocolate, coffee, tea, and pineapple juice. We've had difficulty changing traveller's checks as the hotel and the India Oil man (gasoline supplier for the aircraft) both want rupees as it is Sunday. Finally, the hotel owner, who seems an influential man in Nagpur, agreed to change a traveller's check for us. We took a taxi to his house with his brother and then were all given cups of hot tea with sweet biscuits and engaged in conversation for a few moments after the money and traveller's check exchange. Robin got 800 rupees for $100 and exchanged $200.

We spoke mainly with the head of the family, a good-looking guy of Robin's age with the usual long hair; two other brothers were there also but did not say much. There were numerous other family members in the house. Some young girls and kids were in what appeared to be a sleeping annex to the left of the room on which we sat, and a group of older men sat outside in the shade under the trees. Some women were in the kitchen.

The head of the family said that they had two cars and that he had recently purchased a movie camera (for 22,000 rupees) and a projector on the black market, but had to keep it hidden in case it would be confiscated.

Sometimes he gives it to friends and relations to look after. He told us also that much of a family's money is spent on the wife's jewels (a way to invest).

We then drove to the airport and had to wait until 12.15 p.m. before departure because, although the India Oil man filled us up satisfactorily with gas, he didn't know if he had the kind of oil that we needed (he did have it) and then took a half hour to work out the bill. There is a low standard of general math skills among the working class here. I purchased two 2-rupee and one 2.50-rupee stamps yesterday and was charged 8.50 rupees. Still, we are on our way again now across Central India to Calcutta – a four-hr. flight over similar country to that which we passed over yesterday.

Calcutta (Kolkata)

Flew over part of Calcutta in the Hooghly district and landed at the airport at Dum Dum about 5.30 p.m. After clearing customs, we took a taxi to the large new luxurious Airport Hotel (only two floors of bedrooms completed) erected by India Tourism. Here we got a double bed and a single bedroom for US$30 and ate all our meals in the beautifully decorated coffee shop (slow service). The coffee shop is decorated with bamboo (chairs, etc.) and Indian masks and wall hangings; all dishes were Indian pottery in a wheat colour.

October 13, had large English breakfast and spent the day in the air conditioned room of our hotel. Robin walked to the airport once in the morning. It was very hot and humid, but most of the day we spent trying to get flight permission for Burma. About 5.30 p.m., I took the kids to post letters, etc., and send telex to Thailand Airport. The road was filled with people and so colourful because of all the saris. Also, the India festival, their equivalent of our Christmas, is on now, so music was playing, and there was an amusement park going.

Angela remembers:

Calcutta was full of contrasts. For example, a 5-star hotel had its floor swept with a broom. One of the biggest impacts for me, as a ten-year-old child, was to see beggar children with their legs cut off shuffling around on their stumps. We learned from a guide that it was most likely that their parents had cut their legs off to ensure they could earn more from begging! This blew my mind as a well-protected child who had just lived in the United States for a number of years.

Virginia's diary:

October 14, same as previous day; nearly went up the wall with frustration as Robin booked a call to Rangoon for 11.30 a.m. to see if flight permission to overfly had come. The call was postponed till 3.30 p.m. and then put off altogether because the lines were not working. We decided to go to Bangkok via Rangoon on the fifteenth in the morning, a six-and-three-quarters-hour flight. Robin spoke with the Australian consul in Calcutta and found that permission to fly over Burma had come through the previous day!

Burma

Calcutta (Kolkata) – Rangoon (Yangon) – 5.3 hrs. – VFR
Weather: detoured round thunderstorms

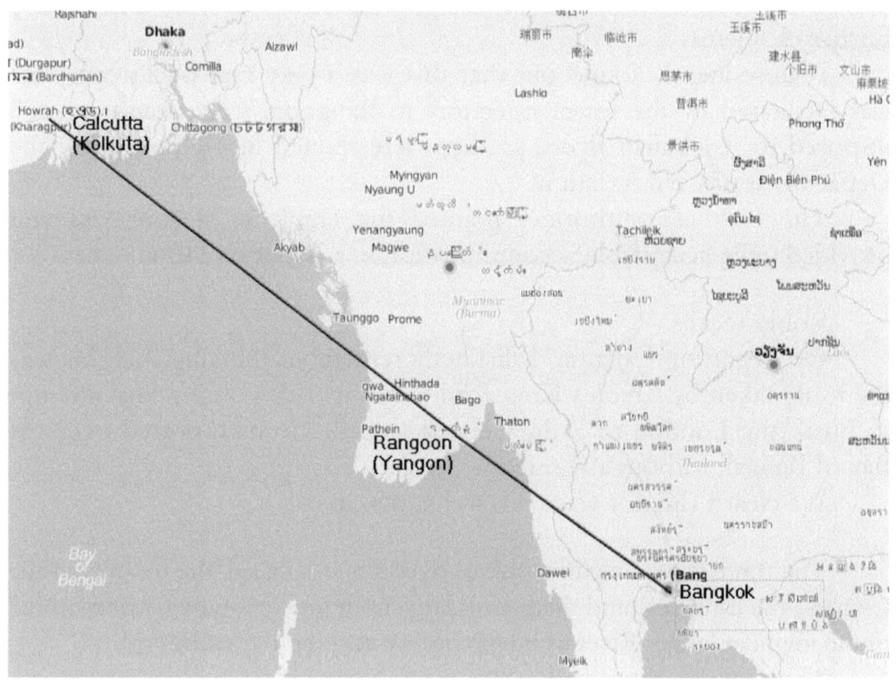

Figure 34 Calcutta (Kolkata) to Rangoon (Yangon) to Bangkok

While we had permission to overfly Burma, we did not have approval to land in Rangoon. A quick calculation of the total flight time from Calcutta to Bangkok, assuming no head wind, was close on nine hours, or right on the limit of our endurance with the cabin tank. A weather check at flight service forecast a head wind of 10–20 knots, which made direct Bangkok non-stop out of the question. What to do?

As Rangoon (Yangon) was on the direct flight path to Bangkok, I guess I took a risk in deciding to depart Calcutta without approval to land in Rangoon.

We had more than enough fuel to get to the Burmese-controlled air space and return to Calcutta, so we departed Calcutta across the Bay of Bengal and then called Burma control on the radio to report as we hit Burma's west coast, as we were required to do. In discussion with the controller, I reported that, because of unexpected head winds, we were unlikely to make Bangkok and requested permission to land at Rangoon. After a delay of about a half hour, during which we were all on tenterhooks, he came back on the radio with the statement that 'Permission is granted'. We headed to Rangoon and landed without any further problems.

I subsequently found out that this was a very rare occurrence that was facilitated by the tower operators in Rangoon, who were very well disposed to Australian flyers, as they were trained in Melbourne by the Department of Civil Aviation.

The Burmese authorities granted the family a 24-hour visa and provided quite acceptable accommodation in a Rangoon Hotel.

Robin recalls:

On departing Calcutta, I distinctly remember thinking that this was the route taken by Charles Kingsford Smith in 1935, on his final attempt to break the London-to-Sydney speed record. He disappeared over the Bay of Bengal, without any trace.

We clearly did not want this to happen to us!!

The route from Calcutta took us over the area called 'the mouths of the Ganges', the estuaries (and there are a large number of waterways or mouths) of the mighty Ganges River as it empties out into the Bay of Bengal.

The Ganges rises in the Himalayas through six major headstream rivers which form five confluences with the mainstream of the Ganges as it flows eastward through northern India and then south-east through Bangladesh to its mouth.

Total length of the river is 2,510 km or 1,560 miles.

Figure 35 Bay of Bengal.

Rangoon (Yangon)

Virginia's diary:

October 15, two more weeks until we arrive in Sydney. As usual, we were up early. We started breakfast at 6.15 a.m. but still didn't get away from the airport until 10.30 a.m. We flew south-eastwards from Dum Dum across green patchwork rice fields and tiny cottages to the delta area of the Ganges. This is massive, partly cultivated, partly underwater, and partly tree-covered. It was all muddy, and Robin thought he spotted some rhinoceros rolling in the mud from 9,000 ft. up.

We are now flying over the Bay of Bengal and will have open ocean for an hour, approximately, before we reach Burma. Weather is clear and good. We did start with a twenty-knot headwind and have been through some rain showers, but no turbulence. Enjoyed seeing the jungles of Burma and arrived 4 p.m. local time. It took two hours to pass through customs and gain a transient visa.

After completing forms, etc., at the airport, we caught a taxi to Inya Lake Hotel – $35 for two rooms for one night. The evening meal in the restaurant was $12! The food was fair. Angela and Stuart are tired of sweet and sour fish, a biting and adult taste, still, different. They had crème caramel to follow. I had mutton mariana, an Indian dish of steamed mutton *served on rice flavoured with sultanas and orange things plus a curry-flavoured vegetable sauce to pour over. Robin had mixed grill. Rowena had an upset tummy and had ice cream.*

Thailand

Rangoon – Bangkok – 3.9 hrs. –VFR

October 16, took taxi to airport early. We were unable to stay longer as the visa was only good for one day. What a pity as Rangoon appeared so attractive, cleaner than India and with less people. We caught glimpses of gold-plated temples and intriguing little shops. Angela and I had our eye on the baskets and soft brooms, but the taxi did not stop. En route to the airport, our driver (who drove an ancient forty-year-old Vauxhall) spoke of life and government in Rangoon. He said the people could not speak against the government. If they did, they would get put into jail. People are not free, and that is not good. It is similar to the communist regime of the day – military rule.

Rangoon is on a river and is not a city of large buildings. Also, there are many trees, so the only thing that stands out and can be seen from a long way off is the magnificent Golden Pagoda (Shwedagon) in the centre of the city.

It took a further two hours before we were airborne and then discovered that Robin did not have his dark glasses, so back to the airport we went. Luckily, they had been found near where the airplane was parked, and so were returned to him. Set off again for Bangkok at noon and flew over water for an hour (the Gulf of Martaban) and land (still Burma), some dense jungle, and then suddenly the great, flat, mostly water-covered plain (Thailand) that is endless canal systems and rice paddy fields.

There is a fascinating viewed from 9,000 ft. as one can see villages clustered at intervals on areas of built-up land or else in the water with houses built on stilts. Wide canals are like highways with barges, large boats and small commuter boats making a busy scene.

Bangkok

Bangkok just happens and is a large city in the midst of the paddy fields. We arrived at 4.30 p.m., and, after the usual customs procedures, caught a taxi to Liberty Hotel – $18 for two rooms, no breakfast – in the heart of the city.

We are hungry, hot, and tired. It was 6 p.m., and so we took a stroll in the street below and found a Thai restaurant (floor show of singing girls also).

We all ordered sweet-and-sour meat or fish and vegetables that came with rice in a marvellous sauce spiced with chillies and accompanied by six different sweet-and-sour sauces to try independently. The kids found this dish a bit hot but nevertheless enjoyed it.

October 17, Angela called this a wonderful day. We were awoken at 6 a.m. by the hotel phone and managed hot Ovaltine at the coffee shop before being collected and taken to where the Floating Market tour ($17.50 for all of us) started at a wharf near the Oriental Hotel. With others, we boarded a launch and travelled along the river (city area) past naval ships, large fishing boats (wooden with unpainted and weathered hulls), and some merchant warehouses and then turned right onto a small canal that was lined at intervals by jungle undergrowth and small wooden Thai houses, some on stilts in the water, others on tiny pieces of dry land (land in Bangkok is scarce and expensive – $50,000–$60,000 per acre).

Then we noticed small boats: some commuter-type motor boats and some an inverted crescent shape that was poled along the canal and carried everything from herbs, meat, fish, water, coal, vegetables, etc., and sometimes a floating restaurant.

We were given a banana each as a sample and then stopped for a few moments to see a silk and carved wooden handicrafts stall. Here we bought an immense pineapple for lunch and played with a baby elephant. We saw more of the colourful market and then stopped by a miniature zoo where we saw monkeys (white and black), an unusual string bear (black with white whiskers and long bushy tail), and another animal that looked like it was half cow and half pig.

We went past more Thai homes and saw the daily life that is lived by the river; it is used for everything except drinking. Then we stopped by the Temple of Dawn for a look. We walked behind the temple and saw another rather beautiful temple and some huge devils. Then we boarded the boat and went home again.

We had a leisurely afternoon at the swimming pool. All the kids have really improved at swimming as a result of having the almost empty pool here and the one in Karachi. We walked the streets while Robin slept.

For supper, we decided to walk in the street below the hotel and to sample whatever was being cooked on sale. We tried hot chilli meatballs, pork and chicken pieces and wings on skewers, tasty little rice cakes, fried bananas, and a quarter pineapple each (unfortunately, it was served with a strong mixture of salt and ginger – not palatable to us, but we brushed that off). It was chopped into pieces, placed in a plastic bag, and given to us on a wood skewer and finished with ice cream and coffee. Then to bed and washing for me. Rob tried to repair his microphone without much success.[11]

Malaysia

Bangkok – Penang – 4.6 hrs. – VFR on top
Weather: detoured around thunderstorms

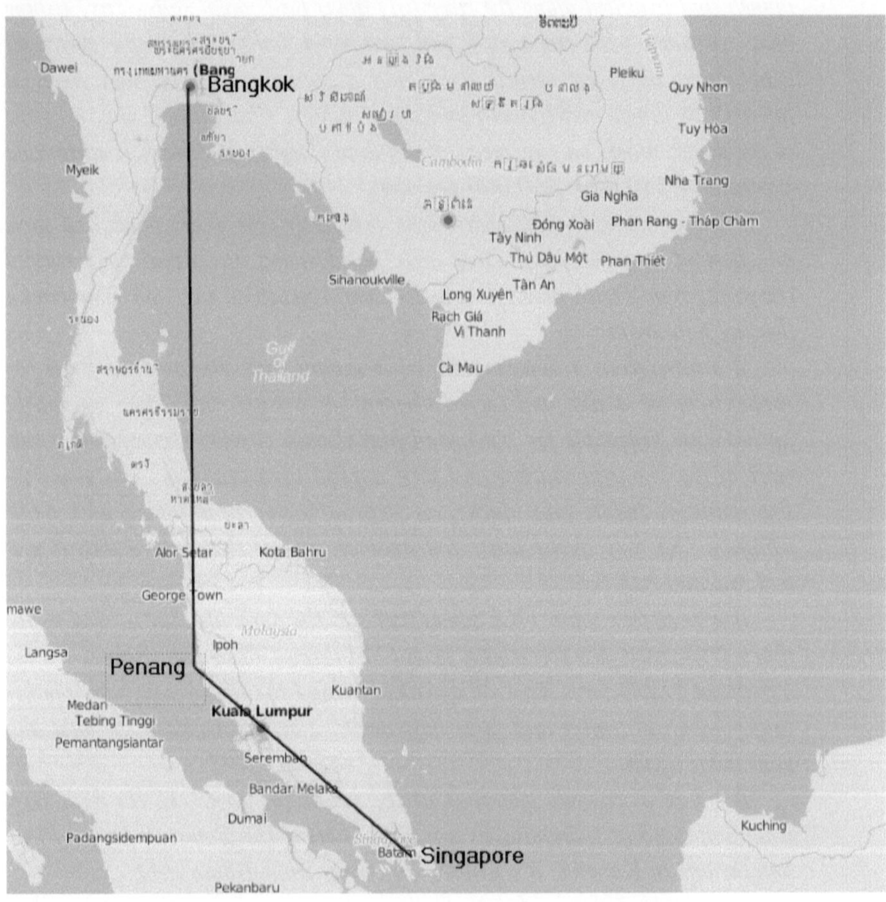

Figure 36 Bangkok, Penang, and Singapore.

---

[11] This was my headset microphone. I had a back-up handheld microphone which I then used for the reminder of the trip.

October 18, departed Bangkok airport at 11.30 a.m. after the usual two hours through customs, flight planning, etc. Angela bought Mrs Ward (her teacher in Massachusetts) a Thai silk scarf of four different shades of blue for $4 at the duty-free shop.

Penang

Set off from Bangkok over the Gulf of Mattapan and down the Burma peninsula. Crossed over and flew down the Straits of Malacca to Penang. In Burma, we saw jungle and what I took to be rubber plantations, although they were not marked on the map. There are more plantations in Malaysia, though not in areas that we pass over. The flight is four hours, and the weather has been good except for rain showers near the Thai–Malaysia border. We enjoyed travelling down the west coast of Malaysia. We saw many rubber plantations, fishing traps in the water, long deserted beaches, and tiny tropical islands. The island of Penang is opposite the Butterworth air base, and we saw some ships, including one gunboat in the straits of water between the island and mainland. We landed at 5 p.m. and, after going through customs and immigration, a brief procedure this time, caught a taxi to the Mandarin Hotel at Georgetown. This was a reasonable price, but the restaurants are expensive here. The beautiful flowers, hibiscus, frangipani, etc., were far more noticeable here than further north. We also saw white sandy beaches and palm trees.

Singapore

Penang – Singapore – 2.7 hrs. – VFR
Weather: departed in rain

October 19, had a short swim in the hotel pool after breakfast before leaving for Seletar airport on the island of Singapore. We had an interesting flight down the Malay coastline. We took off in a tropical rain shower. The visibility was nil, but, after we had finished climbing, conditions improved, and we had a good view of the coastline, rubber plantations, beaches, and mangrove swamps on our three-hour flight.

Arrived at Seletar airport (an army and air force base) at about 4 p.m. and, after clearing customs, took a taxi to Hotel New Hong Kong – bout $35 per night for two rooms. Like the Mandarin Hotel in Bangkok, it was a comfortable hotel. After supper in the coffee shop, we went to bed.

October 20, went to the Indonesian embassy to fill out forms for visa application (this is going to take two weeks). The Indonesian embassy is in a posh part of town that we would like to explore, and the embassy building is new and luxurious. We came back to hotel and bought chicken pies and coconut ice creams for lunch.

Rob then went out to the airport to file a flight plan for the twenty-first and check on several aircraft things. I took the kids on an interesting walk down Victoria Street to the Singapore River past various little Chinese shops. On the river, we saw many 'junk'-type cargo boats loading and unloading goods. We also saw a tent church (Chinese) set up by the river where people left offerings and were praying and burning incense – all very brightly decorated in pinks, golds, and reds. We also saw dragons and dolls.

We bought some cut-up pieces of fruit (pineapple and papaya) to eat and some for Rob and walked back. We bought a handmade loom(S$1.50) from a local hardware shop and then ate delicious fish and chips for supper. We settled the kids down and were collected for a drink by Johnny Moo (a very well-known IT personality in Singapore) at 9.45 p.m. Home at midnight.

October 21, out at airport early. There was no reply back from Indonesia, and Rob and the engineer changed the oil filter on the aircraft. We met a flight instructor from Taiwan (here for two years) and talked for a while. We were all set to go at 12 noon but then had more problems: the Cessna's mike would not function, so we had the avionics engineer look at it. We had just got the mike OK and were taxiing along the runway when word came that our flight plan to Indonesia had not been approved. Back to hotel and square one. Everyone was miserable, including my griping stomach. We had 'gold plated' cheeseburgers for supper and then off to bed.

Angela remembers:

We ended up having to stay for a week while waiting for clearance to travel to Indonesia. We spent a bit of time walking down to the Singapore wharfs to see the junks. We remember all the washing strung along many of the junks as many families lived in them and the terrible smell of sulphur (egg-shells) in the harbour. It is no longer as polluted as it was in the mid-1970s.

October 22, Robin sent two telexes off early today to the high commissioner in Djakarta and Aero International and so far has had no reply. We are just sitting at the hotel and wondering what to do next and how to make the money spin out further. We need to find out the procedures for more money to be sent from the Commonwealth Bank in Sydney.

October 23, contacted Aero International in Djakarta and learned they had not received our $60 for approval to overfly Indonesia (sent from Denmark two months previously). To get approval now requires another $60 and a five-day wait. Everyone is most disheartened at this prospect, but we are determined to sit it out. We moved into one room at the hotel (Dozer on cushions on the floor). A and S sharing one single bed, and Rob and myself sharing the other bed, thus cutting hotel costs in half. We also started eating meals in less expensive restaurants. We walked one-and-a-half miles for a $1.60 English breakfast instead of spending $4.95 at the hotel. Lunch was a fresh pineapple or papaya and some hot snacks or cakes. The $4 supper was eaten in Orchard Road, by day a car park, by night a large open-air restaurant filled with independent barrow merchants who had one- or two-dish specialties ($1.50), cut-up fruit sellers, fried bananas and hot snack sellers, and delicious sate.

October 24, decided we may as well do some sightseeing and so caught a taxi to Jurong industrial estate which was until ten years ago a swamp wasteland but is now a flourishing area of many diverse industries (electronics included), large apartment blocks, and very good amenities such as an ice skating rink that we saw.

We saw from the road the new Polytechnic Institute, which just happened to be at the back of the Japanese Garden that we were planning to visit. This garden is the most beautiful garden that I have ever seen. It was designed by a Japanese professor and given to Singapore to foster friendship. In the middle of the garden are several ornamental ponds, well stocked with carp, and the landscape is done in such a way as to be in complete harmony, each plant with the other. I couldn't begin to describe the vast number of plants and shrubs used (water lilies were exquisite) but did like the way of having a soft-looking shrub or tree next to, in front of, or at the side of something stark or hard such as bamboo. We walked over small orange and red bridges and across stepping-stones and along beautiful paths. We had ice cream in an airy pavilion before summoning a taxi to go back to the hotel HK to await phone calls.

October 25, today we packed our swimsuits and got a taxi and then ferryboat from Jardine steps to the resort island of Santosa. This is also linked to the mainland of Singapore by cable car, but the ferry trip, as well as being cheaper (40 cents to $3), was also a pretty way to go. There was much construction going on here (as in the rest of Singapore), and, because of the high annual rainfall of ninety-five inches, it is always green and has a well-

washed look. We walked to the south side of the island, about one mile, where there is a long and lovely beach and swimming lagoon inside it. We swam and sun-baked all day in the warm and beautiful water and ate lunch at an attractive restaurant nearby. We saw some old flower-covered World War II fortifications on the beach and noticed that all the palms on the beach had just been planted and lots of landscaping done on Santosa. One side of the island is a golf course, and also there is an aquarium.

We ate a delicious squid, prawn, noodle and bean-shoot dinner at the 'restaurant', finished off with large slices of pineapple.

October 26, I was sick all day, and Robin took the kids for several long walks, one right along the shore to see the many ships moored off Singapore.

October 27, another quiet day. Stayed in the hotel most of the time trying to make contact with Mr Schempell of Aero International. We finally got a message to call him on Oct 28 at 1 p.m.

We spent some time at the Singapore Shopping Arcade and also ate some questionable fish and chips there for supper. Robin is nearly ready to jump out of the hotel window with frustration. The kids have been so good during this waiting period and have invented all kinds of games to play. The TV in our room has helped as well.

Figure 37 Filling in time in at the Singapore hotel.

October 28, this must be D-day for us. We ate breakfast at the second-cheapest place ($2.80 for English breakfast) over the road from the hotel, and then caught a taxi to have one last look at the Shore Centre (where Johnny Moo's office is), shopping part of it. We bought three sets of magic markers for the kids ($2 each), and Robin found something for me for Christmas. We returned to the hotel and successfully spoke to Jakarta regarding flight approval. We are going this afternoon.

Indonesia

Singapore – Jakarta – 4.6 hrs.
Weather: flew through heavy thunderstorms approaching Jakarta.

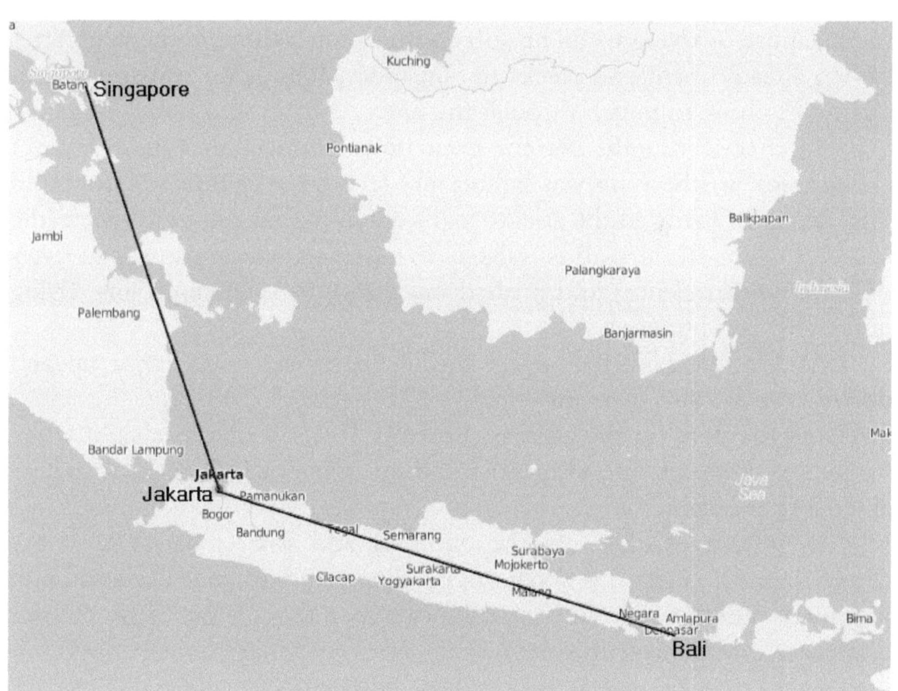

Figure 38 Singapore, Jakarta, and Bali.

Departed Seletar air base at 4 p.m. and are due to land at Jakarta at 8.30 p.m. There was good weather on the trip except for the last hour, when it became dark, and we saw flashes of lightning in the distance to the right of a dull glow that we thought was Jakarta. We missed most of the black clouds but had to go through some terrors just over the city – very turbulent.

Robin slowed down the air speed, and, still, the plane was lifted 1,600 ft. several times in the turbulence. The kids slept all through this. Black clouds were all around us, and I was quite scared and glad to land ten minutes later at the new international airport at Halim. It took only one hour to go through customs and get to our nearby hotel, and another hour to have cheeseburgers and drinks. Then off to bed at 11 p.m.

Jakarta

Approaching Jakarta over the north coast of Java, our flight path was blocked by a line of thunderstorms extending right across the horizon – lightning lighting up the line. I had the choice of turning back to Singapore or trying to find a soft spot to punch through the line. After having already spent two weeks in Singapore, I guess my impatience ran out, and I chose to punch through the line.

After observing the line for some time, I noticed that an area about ten degrees off the nose was lighter and free from lightning. Turning in this direction, I slowed the aircraft right down to manoeuvring speed (the speed at which the aircraft is unlikely to suffer structural damage in cases of extreme turbulence) and pushed on ahead into the cloud line, flying under IFR conditions.

As Virginia said, the severe turbulence tossed the aircraft up and down over a 1,000 ft. many times, while I struggled to keep the wings level and the nose on the artificial horizon. It was a welcome sight when we punched though into clear skies and the lights of Halim airport below and off to the right.

In retrospect, this was the dumbest and riskiest decision of the whole flight. It is just this situation, pushing to get to your destination in inclement weather conditions, that causes most of the light aircraft crashes. We were lucky this time!

Jakarta – Bali – 4.2 Hrs. – VFR
Weather: strong winds and turbulence

The flight from Jakarta to Bali was along the length of Java, from Jakarta in the west to Bali off the east end of the island. Java was formed mostly as a result of volcanic events, as the 'Pacific Rim of Fire' feeds a chain of volcanic mountains forming the east–west spine along the island.

As we departed Jakarta, we flew mostly along the north coast of the island and then headed inland on course for Bali and over two of the highest and most active volcanoes. Climbing to 12,000 ft., off to our right was an active volcano, Merapi, at 9,700 ft. also one of the highest. Merapi's most recent eruption had been three years earlier, with significant loss of life. As we flew over, the volcano was still smoking and would continue to do so until 1985.

Further on, we actually had to deviate around Java's highest volcano, Semeru (12,000 ft.) which had been in continuous eruption since 1967. From our aircraft, we were able to look down into the craters and observe the classic cinder and lava domes and flows down the steep sides of the mountain.

After we passed Semeru, the land dropped steeply away to coastal plains of rice paddies and small villages, until we passed over the south-east tip of the island and headed over the Bali Strait for a left-hand approach to Bali Airport.

Figure 39 Approaching Bali.

Virginia's diary:

October 29, no time to use the swimming pool today. We breakfasted with the Australian and Japanese hockey players who were here for the S.E. Asian tournament, and then went to Halim. We departed Halim at 11 a.m. for the short flight to Kemayoren airport (which no longer exists) where we had to go for fuel and to file a flight plan for Bali. We left Kemayoren at 12.30 p.m., scheduled to arrive at Bali at 5 p.m.

While flying down the Java coast (over the water) and over the idyllic scenery, at first the land looks similar to India, (flat) intensively cultivated, small green fields, and some rice paddies and in between kupangs (villages) with red tile roofs. Close to Bali, we flew over and around several extinct volcanic craters and could clearly see the ridges and valleys down the sides of the mountains caused by once-liquid lava. Now the area is densely covered in green foliage with some rubber plantations in the foothills. tea and coffee are grown locally also. The water along the coastline is blue and very clear. There are numerous small craft on the water near Bali airport.

Bali

We landed at 5 p.m. and caught a taxi in the balmy evening to Ra seaside hotel cottages, a Balinese-type of hotel – $21 for five of us in a cottage, breakfast included. The meals were expensive though – $15 for supper that night – mostly Chinese dishes, tasty but not as good as some we have tasted. We slept well in our unusual red brick and concrete hut with grass roof framed with bamboo. The concrete part was decorated with mouldings in the Balinese manner, and each hut had a tiled veranda. It was a beautiful place to sit in the afternoon and enjoy the fantastic garden or at night to listen to the evening sounds.

October 30, after breakfast at 7 a.m. or so, we went to the beach by the hotel and stayed there until 11.30 a.m. when the sun became too hot. The kids played in the warm water the whole time, just jumping waves. The beach was very good, long, and clean.

School kids attend classes from 6 a.m. to 12 noon here, and, at 11.15 a.m., a group of boys Stuart's age came from the school, stripped off their clothes, and raced into the surf. There were many Balinese sellers on the beach – cool drinks, jewellery, carved items, and bikinis were some of the items that were offered. Robin unfortunately had to go to the airport and re-fuel his plane and change currency and so was not on the beach for so long. Four out of five of us are very sunburned.

Had fresh pineapple and ice cream for lunch and rested in the afternoon, walking a little and writing cards. For dinner, we tried Balinese rice wine, a drink flavoured with sugar cane juice, and more Chinese dishes followed by fresh pineapple and papaya.

Rob is now thirty-seven years old. What a marvellous place to be on one's birthday.

West Timor
Bali – Kupang – 4.4 hrs. – VFR

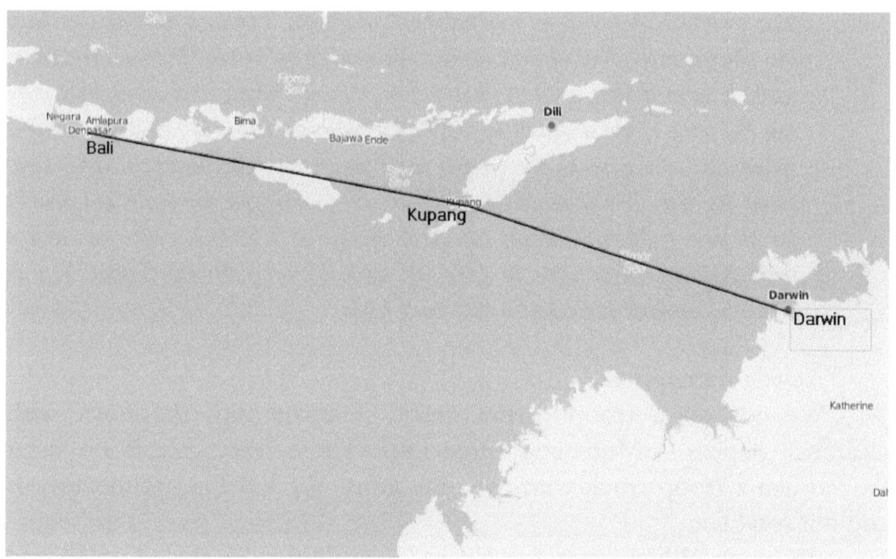

Figure 40 Bali, Kupang, and Darwin.

October 31, the alarm woke us early today, and we breakfasted at 6 a.m. We departed Bali airport at 8 a.m. for Kupang, Western Timor, and a four-hour flight where we will re-fuel and then take off again for Darwin, a further two-and-a-half-hour flight. Most of the flying today is over water, and we are wearing life vests all the time. Next to Java, so our taxi driver told us Bali, is the most densely populated island and has two million inhabitants. Its main industry is tourism.

Kupang

From the air, although it is not easy, one can pick out tiny groups of grass-roofed huts among the vegetation and see the cultivated fields on flat land, but the steep mountain sides and jungle areas don't appear to be inhabited on Bali and the nearby islands.

The time went by quickly until we landed at Kupang, a bituminized coral airstrip adjacent to the town of the same name on Indonesian Timor. Robin re-fuelled here and was charged double the price for gas that used all his remaining US and Indonesian currency and then learned that he had to pay a US$10 landing fee. Then we had to go through immigration and, since the officer had gone off duty (1.30 p.m. now), we had to pay another US$10 taxi ride to Kupang to get our passports stamped. The taxi was like a small bus shared with other airport workers knocking off work. With a shortage of cash, it seemed that we were destined to stay overnight, and our spirits were low (Kupang is not a beautiful place like Bali but rather dry and the people a sullen lot, who gave us the creeps) until we discovered Audrey's $15. That saved the day. We managed to get 'Lousey' Goreng for the kids and drinks for all at a tenth-rate airport café and, finally, at 3.59 p.m., after our return from Kupang, were able to take off and fly out over the Timor Sea to Darwin, another three-and-a-half-hour flight.

Angela remembers:

We got on a troop carrier truck to travel into the town with clearance papers – Mum and three kids. There were guards on what looked like a troop truck with machine guns. We left Dad at the airport and felt total fear.

We were able to pay for clearance with the $5 that Audrey and Keith gave each child as a present before we left. Without being able to pay for the exit tax, we would have had to stay overnight.

I would have preferred to have flown direct to Darwin, but the aircraft range would not stretch that far from Bali.

What we did not know at the time was that Indonesia was about to invade East Timor after East Timor declared its independence from Portugal on November 28, 1975.

Also, what we and the world didn't know on October 31 was that, on October 16, Indonesian troops had already made an incursion into the then Portuguese East Timor and murdered five Australian journalists at the town of Balibo, 10 km into East Timor. The event was to become known as the Balibo Five Assassination, which was also documented in a movie called *Balibo*, released in 2009 at movie theatres around the world.

Although Australia supported Indonesia in its occupation of East Timor – a move that was condemned by the United Nations – whether it was our American accents or the US registration on the Cessna, the attitude of officials and the general population was definitively very hostile. The whole family felt this and could not wait to get back in the aircraft and depart, but we had yet to deal with the customs and immigration officials before we could do that.

When we arrived at the airport, we were told the airport would be closed to departing aircraft at 4 p.m., so when we had the hassle with immigration at 1.30 p.m. and had to go into Kupang to get our passports stamped, we were resigned to trying to find accommodation for the night. We managed to get back to the airport at a few minutes to 4 p.m., started the engine, and were given departure clearance just as the clock struck 4 p.m. We were never so glad to get in the air and set course for Darwin and home!

Australia

Kupang – Darwin – 3.8 hrs. VFR
Night landing

We departed Kupang and turned on an easterly heading to set course for Darwin. We breathed a collective sigh of relief to have 'escaped' from West Timor.

The skies were clear as we climbed to our cruising altitude of 12,000 ft. and relayed our position report and expected ETA Darwin via a Qantas Captain flying overhead at 39,000 ft.

After three hours' flying, first the receipt of the Darwin VOR signal confirmed that we were on course for Darwin and then the town lights and the airport rotating light beacon came into view.

I called up Darwin control to report and seek permission to land, and the welcoming tone and the broad Australian accent of the controller told us that we were nearly home. Touchdown on the runway brought a loud cheer from the back-seat passengers!

Virginia's diary:

> *This was one of the most enjoyable flights I've had. The anticipation of returning to Australian soil must have had a lot to do with it. The kids and Robin were excited too, but Robin was tired, hungry, and irritated by Timorese. Also, he'd not had lunch. We had a pleasant flight with clouds, rainbows, and the sunset being very beautiful, with just areas of slight turbulence and rain.*

Darwin

Robin recalls:

On Christmas Eve, 1974, ten months before we arrived in Darwin, the city had been devastated by Cyclone Tracy, a category-4 cyclone (hurricane) that flattened more than 70 per cent of the city's buildings and killed seventy-one people. This was, up to 1975, Australia's worst natural disaster.

When we arrived, some reconstruction work had started, but, for the most part, the city was a wasteland where commercial and residential buildings had once stood. Fortunately, the Travelodge Hotel was intact and had rooms for us.

The day after we arrived, we all walked around the devastated city and were astounded at the damage that Mother Nature could do in only a few hours. We had never experienced anything like it before.

Virginia's diary

> *Robin's navigation was good, and he just communicated and gave position reports to Darwin through the pilots of commercial flights at higher altitudes until he was within Darwin radio range. Darwin appeared as a long pencil of light, but soon we could see the Darwin airport's rotating light beacon and the runway lights. From then on, things went well with an easy passage through customs and a short trip by taxi to check into the Travelodge in Darwin. We arrived at 10 p.m., making it twelve-and-a-half-hours' travel for the day. All were starving, but we found no restaurants open, so we caught a taxi to The Raw Prawn for takeaway hamburgers 'with the lot' and chocolate milk. We fell into bed exhausted at 11 p.m. Darwin time, 9.30 p.m. Bali time.*

Angela remembers:

We arrived at 11 p.m. to eat a typical Aussie hamburger with 'the lot', including fried egg and beetroot. It was only ten months after Cyclone Tracy, and the city was still flattened.

Virginia's diary:

> *November 1, rest day declared as we'd flown for ten-and-a-half hours yesterday, and the pilot needed a rest. We ate a serve-it-yourself continental breakfast in the hotel bistro, a marvellous place as there is no limitation on amount of food to be consumed so that Stuart got his six slices of toast with honey.*
>
> *After breakfast, Rob refuelled and tidied up the interior of the plane while I sent telegrams and swam with the kids. At 1 p.m., we walked around Darwin and had toasted sandwiches for lunch and then back to the hotel for a sleep and swim before going out for a steak dinner – much appreciated by all.*

Darwin – Mt Isa – 5.2 hrs. – VFR

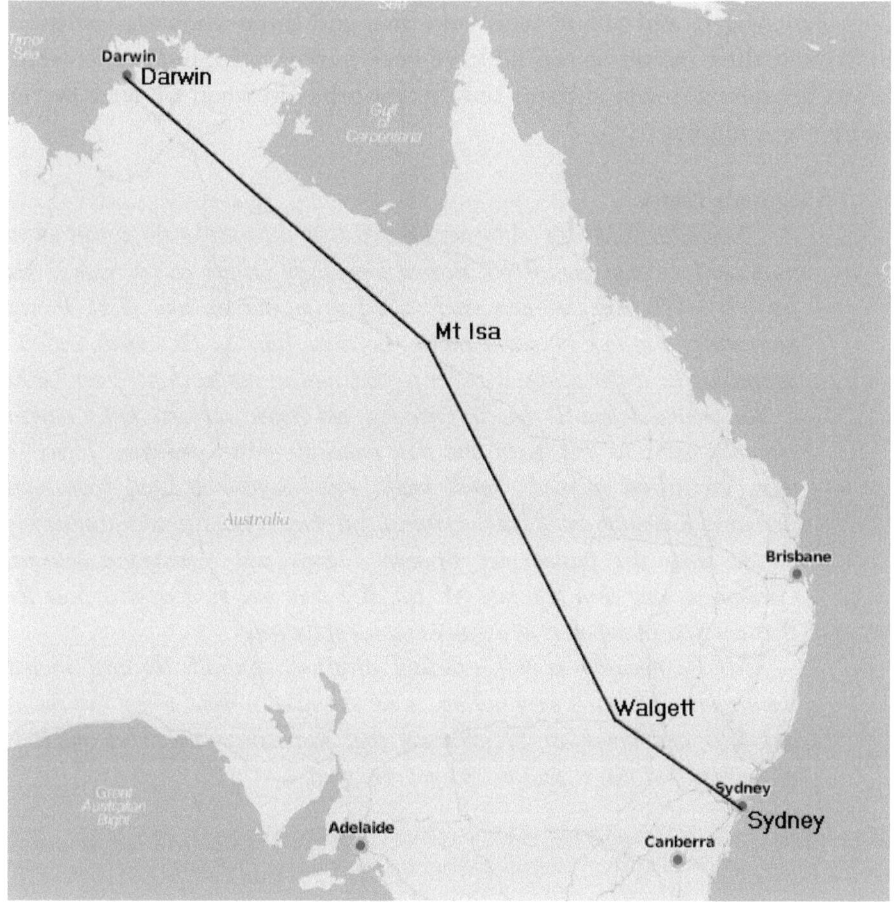

Figure 41 The home leg – Darwin to Sydney.

The flight over the burnt-brown heart of Australia from Darwin to Sydney was uneventful in fine weather conditions.

Virginia's log describes the view from the aircraft better than I could ever do. There were no prominent features except for our amazing perspective on the very large open-cut mines around Mt Isa as we came in to land at the airport.

The Blue Mountains are a very prominent mountain range just to the west of the greater Sydney coastal plains. When we flew over these mountains with their very distinctive sandstone ridges as we commenced our descent into Sydney, the excitement in the aircraft was palpable. For Virginia and me, it was home.

For Angela and Stuart, who were five and three when we last lived in Sydney, their memories would have been very limited, but for Rowena it was her new home as she was only six months old when we were last in Sydney as a family.

Virginia's Diary:

November 2, Mt Isa. After our breakfast, we departed for the airport where we packed the plane and Robin received a pre-flight briefing on his route to Mt Isa. At 10.30 a.m., we were ready to depart on our six-hour flight. It was fascinating for us to see North Central Australia, Barklay Tablelands, with all its vastness for the first time. Weather is good, and we can see clearly from 9,000 ft. the ground below. It has a sameness, red-brown soil and rocks covered everything with, at first, green and then brownish grasses and trees. Every so often, we crossed railroads, small roads, small settlements, and homesteads (including Katherine and Tindal airstrips), but there is not a great deal of variety in the land. We passed over Brunette Downs and Alexandria stations, Camooweal, and then flew into Mt Isa. We were met by a reporter from the Western Star (newspaper) who wanted details of the trip.

Mt Isa township is well-kept and attractive, especially the area around the airport. All hotels were full up, so we stayed at a motel where two rooms cost $26 and breakfast $1. We ate that night in a new Shell roadside restaurant that was expensive and not very good.

Figure 42 Central Australia.

Mt Isa – Walgett – 5.9 hrs.
Weather: cumulonimbus clouds and mild turbulence

November 3, up at 6 a.m. today and at the airport ready to leave at 8.30 a.m. for the five-and-a-half-hour flight to Walgett via Winton, Longreach, and Charleville and then on to Sydney, a further two-hour flight, where I think Rob will have a welcoming committee. He has to call the chief-of-staff at the Sydney Morning Herald (newspaper) from Walgett, and I hope he can get through. The kids are not being good on this, our last, flight, as they are excited about coming into Sydney and have drawn all over each other's faces with magic marker.

This countryside is still very barren. Out of Mt Isa, we crossed the Selwyn Range and an old area of worn-down ridges and flattened peaks (no height) with red soil. We then flew over flatter country, far more greyish in colour (saltbush), some parts sparsely covered with stunted trees. We saw tributaries of the Diamantina River, many isolated stations, and boars and cattle gathered at watering spots or by tree-covered areas.

Sydney – At Last!

Walgett – Sydney – 2.0 hrs. –VFR

November 4, Sydney. After an overnight stop in Walgett, we departed in bright sunny conditions for the short leg down to Sydney. We knew we were home as we came over the Blue Mountains and looked down on the sandstone cliffs and the eucalyptus-filled ravines on our descent into Bankstown airport on the outskirts of Sydney.

There to meet us were Robin's mum and dad, who had flown up from Launceston, and a whole raft of reporters and photographers from the national TV and print media. We are not sure who alerted the press to our adventures, but they certainly turned up in force. We suspect it was Robin's dad when we had safely arrived in Darwin. Before disembarking from the aircraft, we had to wait until the aircraft was sprayed by customs. Perhaps we could have picked up foot-and-mouth disease from one of our European stopovers! Our adventures made national news services that night and front pages of the national dailies, including the Sydney Morning Herald, the Age, the Launceston Examiner, and the Hobart Mercury.

Figure 43 Home at last – Bankstown Airport, Sydney.

Virginia was invited to appear on the *Mike Walsh Show* on Channel 9 TV, and the kids were interviewed at our home for various children's radio shows. No one wanted to interview the pilot …

Aircraft Logistics

Angela, Stuart, and Rowena recall the family logistics in the confines of the small aircraft:

At ages five, eight, and ten, we were typical children on any extended trip with flight legs up to six hours – restless, fighting, and impatient to get there.

Figure 44 Aircraft loaded.

Toilet:

Mum made sure that the last thing we did before we crossed the tarmac to board the aircraft was to 'go to the toilet'. Despite this, of course, we needed to 'go' en route. So with her nurse's training, Mum fashioned a bottle with a funnel for use by both sexes for urination. This was then emptied on the grass as soon as we parked the plane at our destination.

We cannot recall ever having an urgent need for a 'number 2' which could not be held for the duration.

Discipline:

Mum and Dad used the 'carrot and stick' approach to discipline in the cabin. The carrots were a 1-kg bag of jelly beans, initially, then a large package of gum. When that had been consumed, we raided the chocolate bars packed as survival rations with the provisions in the life raft.

The 'stick' was Dad's ruler over the knuckles (corporal punishment was still in vogue!) which he used to plot his course on the charts.

Rowena: On the trip over the Iranian Desert, I remember that Stuart and I were messing up a bit and were obviously causing Dad some stress at an inopportune moment, because he turned round and rapped me over the head with his ruler, which promptly broke in two. Dad's course plotting was shortened from that point on.

Activities:

As with long car trips, we occupied ourselves reading books, playing board games, cards, etc., but for Rowena, in her early reading stage, it was an opportunity to learn her alphabet and practice reading.

We also had four or five books we bought in a Turkish airport (*Aesop's Fables*) that we read over and over again. For a six-hour flight – it was about that long from Bali to Timor – we read all the books five times over.

Angela: During the trip, I started a stamp collection with stamps from all the countries we visited. Compiling this album occupied some of my time between stops. I still have the stamps to this day.

Stuart: I started a coin collection with all the small change left over from our money changing as we travelled between countries. I still have the collection today.

Australia – After the Trip

The Cessna 206 in Australia – Registration

After arrival in Sydney, and assuming we wanted to do more flying in Australia, the aircraft had to be re-registered with Australian registration number VH-RPW. We tried for VH-RPF (Robin's initials), but, unfortunately, it was taken. This was very straightforward as we had purchased the aircraft with Australian specifications.

Tasmanian Trip

We settled back into our home in Wahroonga, Sydney, and bought a new Volvo station wagon. Robin negotiated a new job with DEC in Sydney and signed the kids up for schools commencing in the New Year. Christmas was upon us, and it was time to visit the extended family in Melbourne and Tasmania.

On December 23, 1975, we loaded the family in the Cessna at Bankstown (without bikes this time) and headed down the east coast and across Bass Strait, via Flinders Island, to Launceston, a five-hour trip.

Christmas with the family was great and included a two-hour aerial tour of Tassie for Robin's parents on Boxing Day. We made a short hop to Cambridge airport in Hobart to visit Virginia's family and then up to Moorabbin airport in Melbourne to visit Robin's brother Denis's family. Then it was back to Sydney by January 3. Apart from a few local hops out of Bankstown, this was the last extended family flight in the C206.

The Air Charter Experience

In June 1976, with the C206 gathering dust and eating money at Bankstown, we decided to charter it out to a man named Donald Tait, introduced to me by Rex Aviation, the Cessna dealers. We drew up an agreement for a twelve-month lease, and, with a front-end payment for six months, he turned up in my office to sign the lease and departed with the keys.

Donald had a commercial pilot's license and presented very well. I had no reason to suspect this was other than a legitimate commercial charter. But after about six months, I received a message that Donald Tait was in prison in Bali and that the aircraft was at the airport in Kuala Lumpur.

I telephoned Bali and confirmed Tait was indeed locked up on unspecified charges. As I was planning to head to Europe on business anyway, I flew to Bali, picked up the aircraft keys from Tait, and then proceeded to Kuala Lumpur.

With the help of the people at Bankstown, I was able to source a ferry pilot (there is no shortage of young commercial pilots wanting to build up hours) and arranged for him to pick the aircraft up from Singapore and return it to Bankstown.

A short flight by me from Kuala Lumpur to Singapore, and I was able to proceed on my way to Europe while the C206 returned to Australia in good order and condition.

We had put the Donald Tait incident out of our minds when, in late January 1978, he hit the national headlines after being caught flying an aircraft full of cannabis into north-western Australia.

The following extract from the *Northern Territory News* sums up his history:

> *Donald Tait was one of Australia's most notorious drug dealers who claimed his piece of Northern Territory history in 1978 on a typically steamy wet season day in late January.*
>
> *That was the day the convicted drug runner skidded his light aircraft to a dramatic halt near Katherine with 270,000 Buddha sticks on board.*
>
> *The high-grade cannabis was bought in downtown Bangkok with a street value at nearly $4million.*
>
> *Tait brought his twin-engine Piper Aero Commander to a halt after a daring crash landing in a muddy paddock 14 km north-west of Katherine.*
>
> *He set alight the cargo he had hoped would make him rich and hid in the bush for 41 hours before being found by police, convicted and sentenced in the Darwin Supreme Court to six years and eight months' jail.*
>
> *He was released on parole in 1982 and has since died.*

The unanswered question of course is: Did Donald Tait use VH-RPW for drug running? We knew he had flown the aircraft in Thailand, but I guess we will never know for sure.

Subsequent History and Destruction of VH-RPW

VH-RPW sat at the airport unused for another six months, so, in June 1977, we put it on the market at a price considerably above what we had paid in the United States just two years earlier. In fact, the selling margin more than paid for our around-the-world excursion!

We took it on a short flight to Albury early in July 1977 for a demonstration, and a deal was sealed with a grazier, Kevin Shoebridge, near Albury.

We delivered the aircraft on July 20, and the registration transfer was completed on August 5, thus ending a very exciting period of our family life with an aircraft that had carried us safely around 60 per cent of the globe. It still had only three hundred hours on the clock – not even run in.

Kevin Shoebridge subsequently sold VH-RPW to William Davy of 'Turalla', Bungendore, in NSW on January 6, 1986.

The CASA records show that VH-RPW was destroyed at Bungendore, and the registration cancelled on November 15 that year. Sadly, the plane crashed on take-off from the owner's grass strip on his property, killing the pilot and his two passengers. The analysis from the air safety accident report is shown below.

Analysis - Aviation Safety Investigation Report

The severe weather conditions and the pilot's relative inexperience were considered to be significant factors in the development of this accident.

In conditions such as those associated with strong lee-wave activity, aircraft are likely to experience large airspeed fluctuations and reduced attitude and directional control. It is probable that the maximum climb performance of the aircraft was not capable of overcoming the strong downdrafts in the area at the time of the accident. As the pilot flew parallel to the ridgeline, the aircraft would have remained under the influence of the lee-wave activity.

Whilst the investigation could not clearly establish why the aircraft turned left toward the ridgeline following the abrupt nose-attitude change, it is likely that the pilot was experiencing difficulty in maintaining adequate control of the aircraft and was unable to manoeuvre it to a safer area.

Following the left turn, the aircraft commenced to track downwind. At this time, it was in close proximity to the ground and continuing to lose height. With a tailwind of some 40–50 knots, the speed of the aircraft over the ground would have been approximately 120 knots. The pilot may have been influenced by a false impression of excessive airspeed and a concern about the possibility of colliding with the ground. Consequently, he may have instinctively pulled back on the control column in an attempt to raise the nose of the aircraft into a climbing attitude. Such an action would have further reduced the aircraft's airspeed and may have induced a stall, consistent with witness observations.

Whilst the pilot was familiar with operations from the airstrip and had considerable experience in the accident aircraft, his overall experience was low. It is unlikely that he had encountered such severe weather conditions on previous flights. In addition, he may not have been alerted to the possibility of the existence of lee waves, given the surface winds at the airstrip were not strong and the absence of lenticular clouds above the ridgeline.

Significant Factors

1. The synoptic situation in the area at the time of the accident was conducive to the formation of strong lee waves.
2. The aircraft's flight path was such that it probably remained under the influence of the lee-wave activity.
3. It is possible that, whilst experiencing difficulty maintaining control of the aircraft, the pilot reacted inappropriately to a false impression of excessive airspeed and a concern about the possibility of colliding with the ground.
4. The aircraft stalled at a height from which it was not possible to recover.

Conclusion

After we sold VH-RPW in July 1977, we did very little flying as a family and I allowed my license to elapse in 1978, thus ending a very eventful six years of flying. The one-and-a-half-hour drive from our home in Sydney to Bankstown airport made it nearly impossible to do any regular flying.

What effect did our flying adventures have on the five members of the family in developing their careers and their own families?

Here, as the last item in our book, each of our children records his or her views. Virginia's feelings about the trip shine through in her diary, compiled as we flew the various legs from Boston to Sydney.

Angela's Reflections:

Flying around the world in 1975 was the right time to really open up my eyes. I was old enough, being ten, to take in and understand most of what I saw. I was still young enough and at an age when most children become aware of the world around them that I think it significantly influenced my outlook for the rest of my life.

I learned first-hand over a short three-month period that there were so many different ways of living – and not one of them right or wrong. Diversity became much more than accepting a child of a different nationality with a different way of talking into my school classroom; it meant accepting that whole cultures that were different to mine functioned quite happily and effectively. It also meant understanding that some societies exist with such a big gap in wealth and advantage between the rich and poor – and how lucky we were.

The immediate contrast of seeing so many wealthy European countries and then countries where the disparity in wealth was so stark heightened the impact. In Iran, I was aware of the wealth (from oil) with 5-star hotels and freeways while at the same time struck with the contrast of the donkeys and carts on the dirt roads in Tehran and the carpet weavers going blind in their dark shops from weaving carpets all day. I was also shocked in Calcutta to see a child without legs, begging. It was nearly incomprehensible to me to find out from our guide at the time that his parents had probably cut off his legs so he could earn enough money to look after his family.

The other major impact on me was the sense of security we all take for granted. At the time, I really had a total lack of awareness of what 'military intimidation' means, but years after reflecting on the time we spent in both Iran and Timor (post the Balibo murders), there was a terrifying feeling in both these places that sent shivers up my spine. I know my parents were not deliberately putting us in high-risk situations, but I feel I understood the difference between my safe and secure existence in Australia and other parts of the world.

When I came back to Australia and during my high school years, I felt quite different from my peers. I was always very aware my mother and father had wanted us to value the importance of challenging ourselves and understanding diversity. I felt proud to be a member of a family that had achieved something that was a significant challenge, even though I am not sure people understood what it meant to fly a young family around the world. I felt more aware and outwardly focused on the world. I did not think some of the things my peers felt important were so important to me – such as who my parents were or what they did for a living or whether I went to Noosa for a holiday. And I did not feel that what I had, a great education and family, was a given. And I think that has stayed with me.

My Life

After graduating from Abbotsleigh Girls' School in 1983 and then completing an electrical engineering degree at Sydney University in 1987, I started a career in management consulting with one of the top firms, Accenture. Much of the past twenty years has been career focused. I have been involved in the transformation of big organizations, including Optus and Westpac, and in the outsourcing industry in financial services with EDS and KPMG. I really started with an interest in how technology can help organizations streamline and improve, much influenced, I expect, by my father and his focus on computing.

Over time, however, my focus has been on people change and how to help organizations improve how they deliver services to people. I have found I really like to see the differences in culture in organizations and the way they are structured and what needs to change.

Over the past six years, my focus has been increasingly on applying what I have learned in making change happen in big commercial organizations to helping the public service improve service delivery, in particular in state government services. Recently, I have been working through my own business, Stepchange Consulting, and with small associate firms. And I think this is the direction I want to continue over the next fifteen years. I want to make better use of my skills to improve how services are delivered to the disadvantaged. After having two stints on not-for-profit boards, I would like to continue to invest more time in *pro bono* work.

I married my long-term partner, Tim Fraser, a fellow engineer, in May 1995. Our daughter Ella, now eight as I write these lines, was born in 2002. She is the absolute light of our lives. We enjoy many things together as a family, in particular travel and outdoor sports. And she is now of an age when we are starting to plan some adventures with her in Asia and Africa after a bit of travel in Europe.

Stuart's Reflections:

The family trip flying around the world was not a specific influence in my life in that I have not done anything as crazy or inspiring myself, but I have recently come to see it as the pivotal example of the primary lesson our parents taught us. Namely, that the key to a satisfying life is to challenge yourself with ambitious dreams and apply hard work and perseverance in charting your life towards those dreams. Dreams do not have to be as exotic as my parents' dream to fly around the world; however, provided you are working towards something, the journey will always be interesting.

This was reinforced throughout our lives by examples such as Dad's efforts to build a successful small business, Mum's determination to devote her life to her children's growth, including battling terminal cancer long enough to see her youngest daughter finish high school, and Dad's efforts to rebuild his life after Mum's death and financial hardship as a result of the early 1990's recession.

While all these examples have informed my view on life, it has only been in the past few years that I have realized the subconscious importance of the trip as a reminder that you can achieve anything that you set your mind to.

As I move through mid-life, I have found this trip a valuable reminder when considering how I want to live the rest of my life, while also being convinced of the significance of the trip as a lesson to my young sons on the importance of big dreams and big experiences in life.

My Life

I graduated from Knox Grammar School and then completed an electrical engineering degree from the University of NSW – a major life achievement for me given the intellectual rigor of that degree.

I then moved from an engineering career to business development and general management for the challenge of building businesses and dealing with a variety of different people. I then got involved in international business, travelling extensively in Asia and Europe and living for five years in London.

I have been married for fifteen years to Fiona and am fortunate to have found someone who is great fun and supportive and who challenges me while also helping me to develop and enjoy learning about art, history, and cultures – things that I find very interesting but that do not come naturally to my engineering brain.

I am also extremely fortunate to have two healthy boys who I hope will be inspired by reading this trip book when they are old enough.

Rowena's Reflections:

Every parent tells his or her child that 'you can do anything you put your mind to'; however, not every child is lucky enough to have her parents demonstrate that cliché in such a confident, tangible, and extraordinary way.

As I was so young at the time, my memories of the trip are blurred with the stories and pictures my family shared as I got older. Frequently, Dad would schedule slide nights and test our memories of the trip; unfortunately, I never won the quizzes!

However, the most enduring effects the trip has had on me were translated through my parents in the way they brought me up: a sense of adventure, an appreciation of travel experiences, being able to make choices in life that kept my options open, having confidence to push my personal boundaries, and making decisions that were right for me.

In making a life decision, whenever I was torn between a conventional choice and the right choice for me, Dad always encouraged me to do what was right for me. Convention came second.

With those principles instilled in me, I have travelled extensively and lived in the United States and Canada and studied in the United Kingdom. At times, I have pushed my personal limits physically in sports, from competitive rowing to winter camping in Canada and running triathlons.

Having worked in a range of businesses, I finally had the confidence to admit that I was not made to climb the corporate ladder but rather to regularly look for new professional challenges. I am happy to have been able to forge my life in my own way and fortunate enough to be supported every step of the way by my dad. For that I am very grateful.

One final note, while growing up, our family has always had a strong bond, led by two strong parents. Life has challenged at times, but the fondness and pride we feel when reading this manuscript and sharing the 'trip' story with friends and Dad's grandchildren has energized that bond. That would make Mum, Virginia, very happy and proud.

Robin's Reflections:

Looking back on this period from the security of retirement in 2010, I am very proud of this achievement. I am amazed that after thirty-four years it is still such a special experience in the annals of around-the-world aviation events and grateful that I was able to share this experience with those that I love.

I certainly have no regrets that we decided to fly ourselves home from the United States to Australia in a light aircraft and tour Europe on the way. I know that up to the time of her death Virginia had no recriminations either.

Did we take a significant risk with the lives of our children? Yes, we did. Whether it was a greater risk than piling the family in a car for a cross-country trip in heavy holiday traffic, I will leave for the reader to decide. I do know that I did everything from a training, preparation, and conservative flying techniques viewpoint to minimize that risk. The only 'risky' episode was flying through the thunderstorms on the way to Jakarta.

From a family viewpoint, the experience has been, and continues to be, a great bonding agent whenever we get together for a meal or celebratory occasion.

From a career viewpoint, there is no doubt that I sacrificed a great opportunity in the United States, but the family has, and always will be, the priority, and I am very happy with the way the family has developed.

Acknowledgments

This book could not have been written without the support of many people, both within the extended family and externally.

Angela, Stuart, and Rowena, my three children, have been very supportive throughout this project, both in critiquing the words of Virginia and myself and in the direct contribution through their recollections of incidents on the journey that have added a more human touch to the narrative.

I would particularly like to recognise Angela's contribution in doing the research that identified this journey as still being a unique journey in the annals of intercontinental private flying and in preparing the preface.

Annette, my second wife, has made a major contribution in initially keyboarding the handwritten diary entries of Virginia and then my indecipherable scrawl as I jotted down my thoughts as they came to me. She has also been a great sounding board and proofreader right throughout the creative process.

Tom Stockebrand, my co-pilot on the North Atlantic crossing, has also made a significant contribution with his recollections of incidents and encounters that escaped my attention.

Thanks also to the many reviewers of the manuscript, particularly Liz McQuilken and John Scott, whose attention to the fine detail ensured the accuracy of spelling and grammar.

Last, but not least, I would like to thank my brother Phil for his support in the editing and publishing process.

Robin Frith – February 2011

About the authors

Robin Frith obtained his professional qualifications as an electrical engineer. He was a founder and driver of the Information Technology industry in Australia and the United States for 40 years. He has played an entrepreneurial role as chief executive of two leading IT companies, Digital Equipment (DEC) and NEC in Australia and a Global Marketing role for DEC in the US.

It was during his 6 years in the US that he learned to fly and to develop the confidence to take his family with him on the numerous trips around North America.

After the flight from the US to Sydney described in this book, Robin and his wife Virginia owned and ran their own small business in the computer graphics industry segment for 10 years. This enterprise was wound up when Virginia died.

Over the next 15 years, he held advisory roles in strategic planning for multinational companies on a global basis before retiring from the industry, and with his second wife Annette, returned to settle in the town of his birth, Launceston, Tasmania.

Virginia Frith was born and educated in Hobart, Tasmania, and graduated in 1962 as a Nurse at the Royal Children's Hospital in Melbourne.

She and Robin were married in Hobart in 1964, and were blessed with three healthy children in Angela (1965), Stuart (1967) and Rowena (1970).

She had extraordinary talents in understanding people (and cultures) and meticulous planning skills – which made her a fantastic mother and co-adventurer.

Notes

The definitions below were either obtained directly from *Wikipedia* or were modified with extracts from that source.

---

[i] **VFR** – Visual flight rules are a set of regulations which allow a pilot to operate an aircraft in weather conditions generally clear enough to allow the pilot to see where the aircraft is going. Specifically, the weather must be better than basic VFR weather minimums, as specified in the rules of the relevant aviation authority. If the weather is worse than VFR minimums, pilots are required to use instrument flight rules.

[ii] **ADF** – An *automatic direction finder* (ADF) is a marine or aircraft radio-navigation instrument which automatically and continuously displays the relative bearing from the ship or aircraft to a suitable radio station. ADF receivers are normally tuned to aviation or marine NDBs operating in the LW band between 190–535 kHz. Most ADF receivers can also receive medium-wave (AM) broadcast stations, though as mentioned, these are less reliable for navigational purposes. The operator tunes the ADF receiver to the correct frequency and verifies the identity of the beacon by listening to the Morse code signal transmitted by the NDB. On aviation ADFs, the unit automatically moves a compass-like pointer (RMI) to show the direction of the beacon. The pilot may use this pointer to home directly towards the beacon or may also use the magnetic compass and calculate the direction from the beacon (the radial) at which their aircraft is located.

[iii] **IFR** – Instrument flight rules (IFR) are regulations and procedures for flying aircraft by referring only to the aircraft instrument panel for navigation. Even if nothing can be seen outside the cockpit windows, an IFR-rated pilot can fly while looking only at the instrument panel. IFR-rated pilots are authorized to fly through clouds. Air traffic control procedures and airspace rules are designed to maintain separation from other aircraft. Training is normally done in simulated IFR conditions with training aids such as hoods to help a pilot concentrate only on the instrument panel.

[iv] VOR, short for VHF omnidirectional radio range, is a type of radio navigation system for aircraft. A VOR ground station broadcasts a VHF radio composite signal including the station's identifier, voice (if equipped) and navigation signal. The identifier is Morse code. The voice signal is usually station name, in-flight recorded advisories, or live flight service broadcasts. The navigation signal allows the airborne receiving equipment to determine a magnetic bearing from the station to the aircraft. This line of position is called the 'radial' from the VOR. The 'intersection' of two radials from different VOR stations on a chart provides an approximate position of the aircraft. A 'highway in the

---

sky', along which an aircraft may fly under control of the autopilot or human pilot, may be defined between any two VOR beacons.

[v] Winds Aloft, officially known as the Winds and Temperatures Aloft Forecast (FD), is a forecast of specific atmospheric conditions in terms of wind and temperature at certain altitudes, typically measured in feet (ft.) above mean sea level (MSL). The forecast is specifically used for aviation purposes.

[vi] **ILS** – An instrument landing system is a ground-based instrument approach system that provides precision guidance to an aircraft approaching and landing on a runway, using a combination of radio signals and, in many cases, high-intensity lighting arrays to enable a safe landing during instrument meteorological conditions (IMC), such as low ceilings or reduced visibility due to fog, rain, or blowing snow.

www.ingramcontent.com/pod-product-compliance
Ingram Content Group UK Ltd.
Pitfield, Milton Keynes, MK11 3LW, UK
UKHW041944190720
13854UKWH00004B/1788